SPEAK A WORD FOR
FREEDOM
WOMEN AGAINST SLAVERY

SPEAK A WORD FOR

FREEDOM
WOMEN AGAINST SLAVERY

JANET WILLEN

and

MARJORIE GANN

TUNDRA BOOKS

Published in Canada and the United States of America by Tundra Books, a division of Random House of Canada Limited, a Penguin Random House Company

Library of Congress Control Number: 2014939465

Library and Archives Canada Cataloguing in Publication

Willen, Janet, author
       Speak a word for freedom : women against slavery / by Janet Willen and Marjorie Gann.

Includes index.
Issued in print and electronic formats.
ISBN 978-1-77049-651-4 (bound).—ISBN 978-1-77049-653-8 (epub)

       1. Women abolitionists—Biography—Juvenile literature.
2. Slavery—Juvenile literature. I. Gann, Marjorie, author II. Title.

HT1029.A3W54 2015   j326'.80922   C2014-902487-8
                                                  C2014-902488-6

Edited by Sue Tate
Designed by Leah Springate
The text was set in Bembo.

www.penguinrandomhouse.ca

Printed and bound in China

1 2 3 4 5 6   20 19 18 17 16 15

To our husbands, Mark Willen and Andrew Gann

AUTHORS' NOTE

In telling the stories of people who have fought against slavery, we describe different types of enslavement. By *slavery*, we mean the absolute control of one person by another. We occasionally refer to slaves who were sent by their masters to work for others under a financial arrangement, with the slave paying a specified amount to the master and keeping any money left over. Even though money changed hands, this system is just as much slavery as any other because the slave is still deprived of the freedom to marry, live where he or she chooses, leave one job for another and so on.

Our research led us to historical documents in books and archives and on the Internet. Those earlier writings often use spelling, punctuation and capitalization we no longer use today. We kept the original except where slight changes would make the historical material easier to read. Some quotations from the past include words that are dated or offensive to us today. Obnoxious as these are, they reflect the racial prejudices that underpinned slavery, and we believe they are part of the story we have to tell.

We used many primary sources for Harriet Tubman's stories. Each of Tubman's "scribes" had a different way of recording her speech. In quoting her, we have tried to retain the flavor of her language while smoothing out the dialect to make it easier to understand.

CONTENTS

Elizabeth Freeman is wearing a necklace of gold beads that she later gave to Catharine Sedgwick, the writer who told her story in "Slavery in New England."

CHAPTER I

"To Stand One Minute on God's Earth a Free Woman"

Elizabeth Freeman

I T WAS AN UNUSUAL SIGHT IN THE COURTROOM in Stockbridge, Massachusetts, on August 21, 1781. White people usually confronted other white people at trial, but on that day two black slaves, a woman called Mum Bett and a man known only as Brom, appeared with their white lawyer, Theodore Sedgwick, in a lawsuit against their owner. The case, known as *Brom & Bett v. J. Ashley*, stated that Brom, a "Negro Man," and Bett, "a Negro Woman," opposed John Ashley, their owner. The suit did not dignify Brom or Bett with a last name.

Brom's full name and life story have been lost to history, but we know a lot about Bett from Sedgwick family lore. As a young slave she was known as Betty and then later as Mammy Bett, Mumbet or Mum Bett. Bett married, but there is no record of her husband's name. He died fighting in the American Revolution, leaving her with a young child. Bett took the name Elizabeth Freeman following her court case.

Before the trial, Freeman was a slave in the house of John Ashley, a prominent and widely respected white lawyer. Though Freeman's master was kind, his wife was cruel. The mistress once lifted an iron kitchen shovel, still hot from cleaning the oven, and aimed it at Freeman's sister, Lizzy, a sickly and timid young woman. Freeman did the only thing she could: she jumped in the way to shield the girl and took the blow herself. The shovel cut through Freeman's arm to her bone, burning her and leaving her scarred for life. Freeman often spoke of the incident to Sedgwick's children, and two of them, his daughter Catharine Maria and son Theodore Jr., wrote about it.

"I had a bad arm all winter, but Madam had the worst of it," Freeman later told Catharine Sedgwick. Freeman made a point of leaving her arm uncovered when she was with her mistress so people would ask what happened. "Ask missis!" she would reply, taking the opportunity to shame the woman who had injured her. The mistress never tried to strike her sister again.

More than anything, Freeman wanted her liberty. "Any time, any time while I was a slave, if one minute's freedom had been offered to me, and I had been told I must die at the end of that minute, I would have taken it—just to stand one minute on God's earth a free woman," she told Catharine Sedgwick. One day Freeman heard a reading of the Declaration of Independence, the statement by American colonists that they were breaking free of Britain. Its now famous words "all men are created equal" gave her an idea.

She had overheard Theodore Sedgwick talking with her master on his occasional visits to the Ashley house. Their conversations convinced her that Sedgwick believed that all people were created equal and free. The day after she heard the Declaration of Independence read, she went to his office, told him she was "not a dumb critter," and asked if the law would give her her freedom. Sedgwick agreed to take her case.

Before an all-male, all-white jury, Ashley's lawyers reasoned that Bett and Brom, as they were known during the trial, were Ashley's legal "Negro servants," by which they meant slaves. Sedgwick disagreed. He declared that there was no law establishing slavery and that the new Massachusetts state constitution, adopted just the year before, in 1780, made slavery illegal because it said all people were "born free and equal."

The jury agreed with Sedgwick, declared Bett and Brom free, and ordered Ashley to pay damages and court costs. Once free, Elizabeth Freeman went to work for her lawyer's family in a role Catharine Sedgwick described as a kind of governess. In her later years Freeman worked for other families as well, and "by her extreme industry and economy," her lawyer's son Theodore Jr. wrote, she "supported a large family of grand-children and great-grand-children."

Freeman is the only person not related to the Sedgwick family to be buried in the family plot in Massachusetts. Her epitaph reads:

ELIZABETH FREEMAN
known by the name of MUMBET
died Dec. 28, 1829.
Her supposed age was 85 years.
She was born a slave and remained a slave for nearly thirty years. She could neither read nor write, yet in her own sphere she had no superior nor equal. She neither wasted time, nor property. She never violated a trust, nor failed to perform a duty. In every situation of domestic trial, she was the most efficient helper and the tenderest friend. Good mother fare well.

Following in Freeman's Footsteps

Elizabeth Freeman did something no one had done before. While other slaves had sued on the grounds that their masters had broken a promise to free them, Freeman sued on the more far-reaching principle that slavery was illegal in her state. Her case (along with another that went to the state's supreme court two years later) effectively ended slavery in Massachusetts.

There is no evidence that Freeman called herself an abolitionist, but she was certainly one of the first. By convincing a jury that the Massachusetts constitution recognized her right to be free, she made it possible for other slaves in the state to gain their freedom as well.

Freeman and women like her inspired us, the authors, to write *Speak a Word for Freedom: Women against Slavery*. She was one of a number of eighteenth- and nineteenth-century British and American women—some working together, others working independently on different continents—who had the courage to fight slavery. Their efforts to wipe out a great evil laid the groundwork for today's abolitionists, who are still waging war against slavery throughout the world. Yet when women first took up the antislavery cause, many ran into opposition from men, even from some who shared their hatred for slavery. Like children, women were expected to be seen but not heard. They were not supposed to give public speeches or organize political opposition. Even some women were offended when other women spoke up.

But the women we profile in this book could not be quiet so long as slavery existed. Whether male abolitionists welcomed them or not, they were determined to join the fight to end human bondage. They stood shoulder to shoulder with men—and often were a few steps ahead of them. They knocked on doors to win over allies, came up with the idea of boycotting slave-grown products, organized petition drives, wrote books and evaded slave hunters as they helped runaway slaves escape. As their political action gradually became more respectable, these women exposed slavery as it existed throughout the world and even founded organizations to eliminate it.

Speak a Word for Freedom: Women against Slavery highlights fourteen of these women—some from the eighteenth and nineteenth centuries, and others following in their footsteps today. When we decided to write about women abolitionists, we faced some difficult choices: Whose stories would we tell? We wouldn't have enough pages in the book to profile all the brave women we had encountered in our research. Would we concentrate on one part of the world? On one time period? On the well known or on the little known? Ultimately, we concluded that we could not limit the stories to one time or place or theme—not if we wanted to give a full picture of women's efforts.

We chose some famous women, like Harriet Tubman and Harriet Beecher Stowe, and some not-so-famous, like the pamphleteer Elizabeth Heyrick, the actress Frances Anne Kemble and the runaway slave Ellen Craft. Recent research on Tubman and Stowe has uncovered new facts about them and allowed us to sweep away some common myths. And the courageous behavior of Heyrick, Kemble and Craft—outrageous to many people in the nineteenth century—thrills us today. We decided as well to introduce our readers to two British antislavery campaigners who were active in the early twentieth century: the missionary and photographer Alice Seeley Harris, whose pictures of Congo atrocities are as chilling today as they were one hundred years ago, and the author-activist Kathleen Simon, who shocked Britain by revealing that slavery still existed in places under British control long after her country had abolished it.

Abolitionists continue to shock and surprise us by uncovering the extent of slavery in our own time. The contemporary women we profile perform a range of antislavery work—inside government, in aid agencies and independently.

Some—like Hadijatou Mani, a present-day Elizabeth Freeman from Niger—were once slaves themselves, and all are now advocates for slaves, sometimes facing down thugs and putting their lives on the line.

But why does our book concentrate on women? We want to acknowledge their unique contribution to the antislavery campaigns. Early women abolitionists devised innovative ways to fight slavery. They looked at slave women and saw mothers and daughters like themselves. They also saw that women were made to suffer in ways men weren't. Though both men and women were compelled to perform hard labor, women were forced to produce babies who would be born into slavery. Heyrick wrote that women were especially qualified not only "to sympathise with suffering, but also to plead for the oppressed." Kemble detailed the plight and humanity of women on her husband's plantations, and Stowe was moved by the breakdown of the slave family to write *Uncle Tom's Cabin*. Even now, in the twenty-first century, women are victims of slavery more often than men.

What women abolitionists past and present have in common is their steadfastness as they charted a path toward freeing slaves. When Stowe said the time had come to "speak a word for freedom," the words we selected for our title, she couldn't vote or run for office, but she could use her pen. Modern women have more ways to be heard and to act. The women in this book come from different times and places, but all share Stowe's resolve to banish slavery.

This silhouette is the only known image of Elizabeth Heyrick.

Slaves, like this Jamaican woman, needed British women to plead for them, wrote Elizabeth Heyrick, because no one in their own country would do so.

CHAPTER 2

"No Middle Way"

Elizabeth Heyrick

Two thousand slaves packed into the Baptist church in Falmouth, Jamaica, as midnight approached on a sultry July night in 1838. They sat silently while the British missionary William Knibb pointed to the clock and called out from his pulpit: "The hour is at hand—the monster is dying." As the church bell rang, Knibb announced, "The clock is striking." When the bell's final peal sounded, Knibb exclaimed, "The monster is dead!" The monster—slavery—had finally perished in the British colonies in the Caribbean, freeing the people in Knibb's church and about seven hundred thousand more throughout the British West Indies.

The next morning, Knibb's congregation filled a coffin with a chain, a whip, an iron collar and other punishing instruments of slavery; inscribed it with the words "COLONIAL SLAVERY, DIED JULY 31ST, 1838, AGED 276 YEARS"; and buried it in a deep hole.

Freedom in the Caribbean was long overdue—British abolitionists had been fighting for an end to slavery for more than half a century—but it would have taken even longer if not for the work of Elizabeth Heyrick, a white woman in Leicester, England, almost 5,000 miles (8,000 kilometers) away. She was outraged that slavery persisted in the British colonies, where Africans and their descendants labored without pay, were bought and sold as if they were farm animals or household goods and were whipped and chained at the whim of their owners. Most of the slaves in the British West Indies worked on sugar plantations that enriched absentee landowners living across the Atlantic Ocean in Britain. These businessmen feared an end to slavery would rob them of workers, crops and income.

A politically influential woman like Heyrick was a rarity in nineteenth-century Britain. Women couldn't vote or serve in Parliament, and it was almost unheard of for them to speak publicly at meetings attended by men. But Heyrick refused to sit back and wait while male abolitionists moved slowly to end slavery.

Slavery Pamphlets

In 1824, Heyrick published a twenty-four-page pamphlet with the long name *Immediate, Not Gradual Abolition; or, an Inquiry into the Shortest, Safest, and Most Effectual Means of Getting Rid of West Indian Slavery.* The title itself was an attack on her male counterparts' approach, which was summed up all too accurately in the name of the group they had formed the year before: the London Society for the Mitigation and Gradual Abolition of Slavery throughout the British Dominions.

Pamphlets were to the nineteenth century what political ads and social media are to the twenty-first—a way to reach many people, educate them, persuade them—and the publications were everywhere. Newly mechanized printing presses made pamphlets easy to produce and cheap to buy. People bought them on all the subjects of the day—public health, prison reform, politics and economics. Heyrick's pamphlet on slavery seemed at first to be like the others, an opinion piece on a controversial topic, but there was one important difference: it had been written by a woman in an era when women did not voice opinions on political matters, at least not in public. Heyrick issued her work anonymously, and because of its strong language, readers assumed the author was a man.

Immediate emancipation, or freedom from slavery, Heyrick wrote, "is more wise and rational—more politic and safe, as well as more just and humane." Appealing to religion, reason and justice, she rebutted the men's arguments for a slow approach to ending slavery, point by point.

Some men said slaves shouldn't be freed until they became fully Christian, which would take time. But Heyrick believed that slaves would never adopt Christian teachings so long as their teachers violated "the spirit and letter of the Christian religion" by supporting slavery.

Some men said newly freed slaves wouldn't continue their work on plantations, thus stopping the production of sugar and disrupting the British economy.

She disagreed. "It has been abundantly proved that voluntary labour is more productive, more advantageous to the employer than compulsory labour," she wrote.

Heyrick could also point to the glaring failure of an earlier attempt at gradual emancipation. When Parliament passed a law shutting down the British transatlantic slave trade, which shipped captured Africans to Europe and North America, abolitionists thought it would be the beginning of the end for slavery, but seventeen years had passed and slavery continued unchanged.

Heyrick believed that freedom was an absolute right, and that people were being held as slaves so plantation owners could maintain a rich lifestyle. "Must hundreds of thousands of human beings continue to be disinherited of those inherent rights of humanity . . . [so] that a few *noble lords* and *honourable gentlemen* may experience no privation of expensive luxury?"

Reviews of the pamphlet were good, and it quickly went into three editions in Britain, with the men's antislavery society buying twelve copies. The pamphlet also made it to the United States, where it had an equally strong impact. "Who first gave to the world the doctrine of immediate emancipation? It was a woman of England—Elizabeth Heyrick," wrote the American abolitionist William Lloyd Garrison.

Heyrick also spread her views in a monthly publication called *The Humming Bird; or, Morsels of Information on the Subject of Slavery* that she produced with two friends, one of whom may have been her sister, Mary Ann. The three did not disclose their names, but admitted to being women and appealed directly to other women. And they left no doubt about their opinion on slavery: "This is a cause in which we must *conquer or die*. There is no middle way."

But Heyrick was convinced that words alone would not free the slaves. She announced a "more decisive, more efficient" scheme: a mass boycott of slave-produced sugar. "When there is no longer a market for the productions of slave labour, then, and not till then, will the slaves be emancipated," she wrote. She called on everyone to take a side: "[T]he whole nation must now divide itself into the *active supporters* and the *active opposers* of slavery."

To enlist those active supporters, Heyrick joined with a few friends in forming the first women's abolitionist society, the Female Society for Birmingham, in 1825. Enthusiasm spread from household to household as women knocked on doors, visiting other women, inviting them to join associations and urging them not to buy sugar produced by slaves. In 1825 in Leicester alone, fifteen hundred families—a fourth of the population—agreed to abstain from slave-grown sugar. By 1833, more than seventy ladies' associations were promoting the boycott throughout Britain. In the town of Worcester, women refused to purchase West Indian sugar, even boycotting bakers who used it and shopkeepers who sold it.

Careful as Heyrick and the other women were to portray their work as charitable—since political action was still reserved for men—they were nonetheless attacked for overstepping their bounds. One outspoken critic was the politician William Wilberforce, who had led the campaign in the British Parliament to end the slave trade some forty years before. Just as Heyrick approached the question of slavery from a Christian perspective, Wilberforce looked at the women's actions from a religious perspective—but he didn't approve. "[F]or ladies to meet, to publish, to go from house to house stirring up petitions—these appear to me proceedings unsuited to the female character as delineated in Scripture," he said.

Young Humanitarian

Elizabeth Heyrick was not to be deterred by the disapproval of Wilberforce and others like him. Even when she was a child, she let her conscience guide her. When all but the prettiest of a litter of kittens were to be destroyed, young Elizabeth cried that the ugliest should be the one spared because it had no one to speak up for it. "So earnest and so determined was she to save the poor little fright," her brother Samuel Coltman recalled, that the decision was made to save two—the prettiest and the ugliest.

A friend told another story of young Elizabeth's humanity. Given twopence to buy gingerbread, she was stopped by a beggar and decided to give him half her money. And in an early sign that moderation wasn't her style, she turned back a moment later and gave the beggar the remaining coins as well.

Though she cared about the less fortunate, Elizabeth was quite fortunate herself. Her father was a successful cloth manufacturer, and she was a talented painter and a strikingly attractive young woman, though a bit vain and proud. "My eldest sister Elizabeth grew in stature, as in beauty," her brother Samuel wrote. "She was a high-spirited child and had early symptoms of pride and self-will."

In her teens, Elizabeth met John Heyrick, a dashing young lawyer known as the Apollo of the Town. "She saw; she loved, and was beloved. It was all the work of a moment," a friend wrote, and in 1789 they married. But one June evening eight years later, Elizabeth returned from a church service to find her husband dead of a heart attack, leaving her a childless widow.

John Heyrick's death prompted a period of soul-searching, and Elizabeth began to deny herself pleasures and focus her attention on others. Her father gave her an allowance, but she kept little of it, spending much of the money on the needy. She visited hospitals, the poor and prisons, even paying prisoners' fines for minor crimes, like hunting on private land.

Faith at Work

In 1802, Heyrick acted against her mother's advice by opening a girls' boarding school in her home. She also opposed her mother's wish that she employ a servant. "I can only say that it is not my disposition to impose burdens on any of my fellow creatures," she wrote.

Heyrick converted to her husband's religion, Methodism, when she married, but in 1807 joined the Leicester Society of Friends. The Friends, commonly known as Quakers, shared her conviction that all people were equal, regardless of their sex, race or social class. At a time when most religions favored men, the Friends treated both sexes as equals. Heyrick shared her faith's commitment to prison and hospital reform, nonviolence, improved working conditions in factories and the abolition of slavery.

Heyrick tackled all of these topics in her pamphlets. She published the first around 1805, warning against wars, which she believed people mindlessly rushed to support. Opposition to bloodshed prompted her next pamphlet too, but this time it was animal blood. In the town of Bonsall, Derbyshire, she and her sister witnessed people engaged in bull-baiting, a popular sport in which dogs attacked a chained bull. The women intervened, hoping to stop the torture, but when that proved unsuccessful, Heyrick bought the bull and hid it in a woman's parlor until the bloodthirsty crowd dispersed.

She wrote two pamphlets against bull-baiting and distributed them in Bonsall, gaining full support from the local clergyman, who achieved at least a temporary ban. Heyrick is credited with ending the pastime altogether in another town, Uppingham, Rutland. Bull-baiting became illegal in all of Britain in 1836.

Heyrick continued working for the church, running her school and writing pamphlets. She urged prison reform, opposed bull-baiting and other forms of cruelty to animals, decried capital punishment and instructed children. She allied herself with striking weavers in Leicester, although it meant opposing her brother John, a factory owner. She published a total of eleven pamphlets and books before *Immediate, Not Gradual Abolition* in 1824, and over the next four years, she released at least eleven more publications, most anonymously, including two books for children. Heyrick devoted seven pamphlets to the subject of slavery, advocating an end to the "national disgrace."

Of all her writings, *Immediate, Not Gradual Abolition* was the most influential, but her later pamphlets expanded on her antislavery views and addressed different readers to gain their support. An 1828 pamphlet, for example, spoke directly to women, saying the "peculiar texture of [a woman's] mind, her strong feelings and quick sensibilities, especially qualify her, not only to sympathise with suffering, but also to plead for the oppressed."

Women were discovering that they had clout, and not only through the sugar boycott. Their antislavery societies contributed financially to men's groups. Heyrick's group, the Female Society for Birmingham, was one of the largest. In 1830, it took a strong stand against the men's organization based in London because that group did not support immediate emancipation. The women informed the men that they would not give them any money unless they abandoned their gradual approach and stopped supporting resolutions in Parliament that would delay emancipation.

Seven weeks later, the men's group dropped the words *mitigation and gradual abolition* from its name, becoming the London Anti-Slavery Society and committing itself to the "entire abolition" of slavery.

"Women Did Everything"

Public opinion was certainly on the side of immediate emancipation, and women were being listened to. Once so reluctant to speak out publicly that they didn't even sign petitions, women now signed in the hundreds of thousands. An 1833 petition was the largest and inscribed only by women. Delivered on May 14, the day the Slavery Abolition Act was introduced in the House of Commons, the petition bore 187,157 women's signatures, which had been collected in only ten days. It was "a huge featherbed of a petition," the prominent abolitionist George Stephen said—so big that it was "hauled into the House by four members amidst shouts of applause and laughter."

One signature not on it was that of Elizabeth Heyrick. She had died less than two years earlier, in October 1831—too soon to see slavery come to an end, and too soon to be disappointed in the law. It did not promise immediate emancipation. Children under six years of age were to be freed on August 1, 1834, but others had to work for their masters as apprentices for another six years (later shortened to four), their lives little different from what they'd been. While the slaves would receive no money for their long years of unpaid labor, planters were to be reimbursed for their "property" losses—the slaves. Those who lost the greatest number of slaves would receive the most money, which for some would be the equivalent of tens of millions of dollars in today's currency.

With the passage of the law, even men began to recognize the importance of the women's activism. As George Stephen acknowledged: "[Women] did every-thing. . . . They circulated publications: they procured the money to publish; they . . . talked & coaxed & lectured: they got up public meetings & filled our halls & platforms when the day arrived; they carried round petitions. . . . [T]hey formed the cement of the whole Antislavery building."

At the forefront of those British women was Elizabeth Heyrick. Without her vigorous words and strong arguments, her visits to neighborhood women, her high principles and self-will, women may not have banded together to boycott sugar and arouse public opinion to push for a speedy end to slavery, and the monster would not have died in the British West Indies in 1838. And without her determination, today's activists might not be as effective in calling attention to injustice. Anyone who goes door to door with a petition, supports a boycott, signs a petition, sends a Tweet to champion a political cause or writes an opinion column is following her example.

Portraits of Ellen Craft in disguise, though without the bandage on her face, were big sellers and helped the couple raise money.

ELLEN CRAFT,
The fugitive Slave.

William Craft

Ellen Craft

CHAPTER 3

"I Had Much Rather Starve in England, a Free Woman"

Ellen Craft

ELLEN CRAFT ROSE TO ADDRESS more than eight hundred well-wishers seated in the Court Street meetinghouse in Newburyport, Massachusetts. The year was 1849, and she was dressed like the women of her day, in a long skirt that fell gracefully to the floor. Only four months earlier, in December 1848, she had looked very different—with short hair, white shirt, necktie, jacket, trousers, tall hat and boots. Disguised as a white man, she had joined her black husband in a daring escape from slavery in the South to freedom in the North.

But by the time she rose to speak before the sympathetic audience that April night, Ellen and her husband, William, had become two of the most celebrated fugitives in the Northern United States and two of the most infamous in the South. Crowds in Massachusetts thronged to hear "the Georgia fugitives," and at a time when women rarely spoke in public, people called out for Ellen's voice.

Ellen didn't set out to become a hero or an antislavery lecturer. Her aim had simply been to flee slavery so that any children she had would be born in freedom. But the story of the Crafts' dramatic escape to Pennsylvania, with Ellen disguised as a white slavemaster and her husband as his devoted black slave, captivated the antislavery community and thrust the couple onto the public stage. The abolitionist newspaper *The Liberator* reported that Mrs. Craft recounted their escape "in so simple and artless a manner as must have carried conviction to the mind of everyone present." Whether she had planned it or not, Ellen Craft had become an abolitionist, one of the most popular in the United States and later in Britain, with audiences clamoring to see her.

Slave Years ▶━◼▬◼━◼▬◼━◼▬◼━◼▬◼━◼▬◼━◼▬◼━◼▬◼━◼

Ellen was born in 1826. Her father was Major James Smith, a white plantation owner in Clinton, Georgia; her mother, Maria, was an African-American slave. Under Georgia law, that made Ellen, like her mother, the property of the major and his wife, Eliza, whom Ellen called an "incessantly cruel" mistress.

Ellen was so fair-skinned that people often assumed she was one of the Smiths' own daughters. This mistake offended the mistress, provoking her to exile the child from her home by giving her as a wedding present to her eighteen-year-old daughter, also named Eliza. The move sent Ellen to Macon, Georgia—12 miles (19 kilometers) from her mother, a considerable distance in the days before automobiles and telephones.

William Craft, an African-American slave, was also living in Macon. Craft's owner sent him to a cabinetmaker's shop to learn the trade. He could keep some of the money he earned but had to give his owner $220 a year, a princely sum in those days, and pay for his own food and lodging. Like Ellen, William knew what it was to be separated from his family; his first owner had sold away William's mother, father, sisters and brothers one by one.

Ellen and William fell in love and talked about marriage, but unlike white Southern couples, who dreamed of a happy future with children of their own, slaves knew dreams could be nightmares. Their lives were not their own: they were in the hands of their master, who could deny them permission to marry and even sell them or their children without giving them a moment to say good-bye.

Ellen and William postponed their marriage for years in the futile hope that they could wed in freedom. "My wife was torn from her mother's embrace in childhood, and taken to a distant part of the country," William wrote in *Running a Thousand Miles for Freedom*, the narrative of his and Ellen's escape. Ellen had seen so many parents and children parted this way "under the wretched system of American slavery" that the possibility filled "her very soul with horror." William was determined to find some way to "escape from our unhappy condition, and then be married."

The nearest state where slavery was illegal was Pennsylvania, approximately 1,000 miles (1,600 kilometers) from Georgia, past South Carolina, North Carolina, Virginia, Maryland and Delaware. At a time when slaves needed their owners' permission just to leave home, the distance seemed insurmountable, and the punishments if they were caught included separation, beatings, hard labor, even death. "[N]othing seems to give the slaveholders so much pleasure as the catching and torturing of fugitives," William wrote.

Discouraged about finding an escape route, they married in 1846, though slave weddings weren't recognized under Georgia law. As a lady's maid and a cabinetmaker, the two were privileged, with freedoms denied to most American slaves. Ellen had a one-room cottage in the woods where, when her owner didn't need her, she could live privately with William. Their unusual independence opened the possibility of slipping away without being noticed immediately. By December 1848, William and Ellen had devised a plan.

Secret Plan

The light-skinned Ellen would disguise herself as a white gentleman, the son of a plantation owner, and William, whose skin was darker, would be his slave, attending him en route to Philadelphia, a large city in Pennsylvania, to seek a cure for the master's rheumatism. (This pretense was necessary because no white woman would travel alone with a black man, even if he were her slave.)

Ellen's work as a maid brought her close to slaveholding whites, and she observed them carefully. She knew how they liked to dress for travel, could imitate their manners and the way they spoke, and understood their way of thinking. This would make it easier for her to pass as a white. William's financial arrangement with his owner let him save enough money to buy everything Ellen needed to transform her appearance and to pay their expenses during the trip.

To engineer a flawless escape, the couple had to think of all the obstacles they might meet along the way. In Georgia, a slave could not travel freely without a permit from his or her master. So Ellen and William told their owners that Ellen wished to visit a sick relative several miles away, and as trusted slaves, they got the passes they needed. Ellen also realized that she would have to sign her name in hotel guest books and at the customs house in Charleston, South Carolina—but as a slave, she had never learned to read or write. She decided to put her right arm in a sling so she'd have an excuse not to write. Her skin was too smooth to look like a man's, she knew, and her face and eyes might show that she was nervous. She decided to hide her beardless face with a bandage, to look as though she had a severe toothache, and conceal her eyes with green-tinted glasses. And if William supported her whenever she walked and treated her arm with a cream to ease the "rheumatism," she would appear to be severely crippled by her illness. The people they met on their journey would understand why a traveler in so much pain wouldn't want to engage in friendly conversation with them.

Before dawn on December 21, 1848, William cut his wife's hair short, helped her dress in men's clothing and applied the bandages to her face and arm. Ellen was now William Johnson, the white planter's son whom William Craft would accompany from Macon, Georgia, to Philadelphia, Pennsylvania, and from slavery to freedom.

Destination Freedom

For four days, Ellen and William had to act their parts—on train cars, on steamers, at hotels and in horse-drawn buses. A wrong word or turn of bad luck could spell an end to their hopes. They would have many narrow escapes during their flight to freedom, but the first came before their train even left the station, when William spotted his boss from the cabinetmaker's shop. William hid his face as the man interrogated the ticket seller, then peered into carriage after carriage, all in search of his slave, who he rightly suspected was "[making] tracks for parts unknown." Just in time, the bell sounded and the train pulled out of the station.

While William was breathing a sigh of relief, Ellen—in a first-class car—was suddenly alarmed. Sitting beside her was someone she recognized, a man who had been a dinner guest at her owner's home the night before and who knew her from childhood. Even if he couldn't place her face, he might recognize her voice and identify her as a runaway. To make matters worse, the man wanted to draw her into conversation. Thinking fast, Ellen pretended to be deaf, which irritated the man, who shouted at the top of his lungs, "It's a very fine morning, sir!"

"Yes," she finally replied, but when she turned away, a fellow passenger commented that it was a terrible thing to be deaf, and the man soon gave up on Ellen and turned to the other travelers for more interesting conversation.

Though Ellen didn't speak, she did listen, and as talk turned to the subject of abolitionists, she learned. As a house slave, Ellen had overheard whites describe abolitionists as some "fearful kind of wild animal," but as she listened closely to what the neighboring passengers said, she realized that abolitionists were really her allies. They were the people who wanted her to be free.

Fortunately, her owner's friend left the train at the first stop. Now seated with strangers, Ellen could breathe more easily, though she still spoke little throughout the journey.

Ellen and William remained on the train until they reached Savannah, Georgia, where they boarded a steamer for Charleston, South Carolina. When her fellow passengers learned that her destination was Philadelphia, they warned Ellen (the person they believed to be William Johnson), in coarse language that reflected the racist feelings behind America's system of slavery, that her "slave" would take advantage of the move to try to escape. "You have a very attentive boy, sir; but you had better watch him like a hawk when you get on to the North. . . . I know several gentlemen who have lost their valuable niggers among them [damned] cut-throat abolitionists," warned the ship's captain.

In Charleston, Ellen and William had a short time to themselves in a hotel before they had to face registering in the customs house. Charleston was a hub for slave trading, and authorities closely monitored the movement of blacks to ensure that no slaves escaped. People who wanted to travel out of the state with a slave had to convince officials they had the right to do so. Then they signed a registry book and paid a fee.

Just as Ellen had expected, there were problems. When the official asked her to sign the log, she pointed to her bandaged hand and asked him to initial it for her. The clerk shook his head and said, "I shan't do it." Other passengers began to stare at them, making Ellen uncomfortable. Fortunately, a man who recognized her from the steamer out of Savannah stepped forward and said, "Mr. Johnson—know his kin like a book." To Ellen's relief, that caught the attention of the steamer's captain, who said he'd vouch for the passenger and signed the book on "Mr. Johnson's" behalf.

From Charleston, they took steamers and trains with frequent stops and transfers, and they met new people at each one. Even friendly encounters posed some risks. On the train ride to Richmond, Virginia, two sisters boarded the car with their father. They noticed the handsome invalid, made a pillow for his head from their shawls, covered him with his coat and spoke warmly about him when he appeared to be asleep. "Papa," one said, "he seems to be a very nice young gentleman." Declared the other, "Oh! dear me, I never felt so much for a gentleman in my life!" Before leaving the train in Richmond, the father presented the invalid with a recipe to cure rheumatism. Ellen thanked him and rushed to put the paper in her pocket, afraid she might hold it upside down if she pretended to read it.

Throughout their long trip north, Ellen had to appear to agree with the white passengers, no matter how bigoted, hateful, ignorant and illogical they were. She let down her guard only once, when a widow claimed that William was her slave Ned, who'd escaped eighteen months earlier. "I never in my life saw two black pigs more alike than your boy and my Ned," the widow said.

The woman wanted Ned back, but she didn't think well of him or any slave, calling them all ungrateful, worthless and troublesome. The worst thing you could do was emancipate them, she said. Her husband had freed his slaves in his will, she explained, "But I and all our friends knew very well that he was too good a man to have ever thought of doing such an unkind and foolish thing, had he been in his right mind, and, therefore we had the will altered as it should have been in the first place."

Furious that the man's slaves had been cheated of their freedom, Ellen couldn't restrain herself. "Did you mean, madam, that willing the slaves free was unjust to yourself, or unkind to them?" she asked.

Unkind to them, the woman replied. It would be so cruel to turn them loose, she added, "when there are so many good masters to take care of them."

Ellen said no more, not wanting to draw further attention to herself.

Their next stop, Baltimore, was the last major port in the slave states, a place where railway officials kept a close eye out for runaways. (If they let any pass from Baltimore to Philadelphia, they would have to reimburse the slave's owner for his lost property.) A conductor asked William his destination, and told him to have his master report to the train office. As "Mr. Johnson's" slave, William was under suspicion. Just hours from the free city of Philadelphia, Ellen had to perform her final act.

She stepped into the role of a haughty Southern aristocrat, used to getting his own way, unwilling to take no for an answer and impatient with clerks and other servants. When a railway conductor told Mr. Johnson, "It is against our rules, sir, to allow any person to take a slave out of Baltimore into Philadelphia, unless he can satisfy us that he has a right to take him along," Ellen was adamant. "I bought tickets in Charleston to pass us through to Philadelphia," she asserted, "and therefore you have no right to detain us here." The official stood his ground, and neither of them spoke for a minute. But when the bell rang, signaling the train's imminent departure, the official relented. "I really don't know what to do; I calculate it is all right." Ellen had acted her part well.

The hours passed slowly until dawn approached, and finally Ellen and William saw city lights and heard a passenger call out, "Wake up! We're at Philadelphia." It was Sunday, Christmas Day 1848, and Ellen and William were tasting freedom for the first time.

In the North

The Crafts' immediate destination was a boardinghouse that William had heard about on the last leg of their journey to Philadelphia. The house's owners, opponents of slavery, gave them a warm welcome but warned them against staying there long. Though Pennsylvania was a free state, slave catchers from the South would scour the streets of Philadelphia for fugitive slaves, earning good money for any they captured and returned to their owners in the slave states. For their safety, Ellen and William lived for a few weeks 25 miles (40 kilometers) outside the city, with a white antislavery family who began to teach them to read and write. While there, the family introduced them to leading abolitionists, including William Wells Brown, the man who would guide them toward their future career.

Like the Crafts, Brown was an escaped slave. Fifteen years earlier, he'd fled his owner in Missouri, and since then he'd taught himself to read and write, gaining fame as a successful songwriter, autobiographer and antislavery speaker. Here was a man Ellen and William understood, with a background they shared and a self-confidence they admired. Brown urged them to join him on the lecture circuit in New England, knowing that their story, coupled with Ellen's appearance, would excite audiences. At a time when a speaker's color—black, brown, white or any other shade—was at least as important as his or her words, Brown knew that Ellen's light skin would elicit sympathy from her audience. Everything Brown suggested to them was new—a lecture tour throughout New England, standing in front of hundreds of people—but they listened and said yes.

Even before he left Pennsylvania, Brown trumpeted Ellen and William's daring escape in a letter he sent to William Lloyd Garrison, the abolitionist publisher of *The Liberator*. He urged the newspaperman to inform the public, and he proclaimed Ellen "truly a heroine."

Abolitionists on the lecture circuit were part entertainer, part educator, part politician. With their eloquent language, appeals to religion and powerful stories, they asked their audiences to work with them to eradicate slavery. When Ellen and William teamed up with William Wells Brown, they joined one of the most popular abolitionists of the time.

Together they traveled to sixty towns in Massachusetts and were cheered wherever they appeared. It was usually only Brown and William who spoke, not Ellen. Men and women followed clear rules in the mid-1800s, and those rules told women to be domestic, passive, religious and pure. To speak in public was not considered ladylike. But it was often Ellen people talked about. "Ellen Craft, the young wife, is a woman who may well be called beautiful," the white abolitionist Samuel J. May wrote to an English friend. He explained:

She has no trace of African blood discernible in her features—eyes, cheeks, nose or hair, but the whole is that of a Southern-born white woman. To think of such a woman being held as a piece of property, subject to be traded off to the highest bidder (while it is in reality no worse or wickeder than when done to the blackest woman that ever was), does yet stir a community brought up in prejudice against color a thousand times more deeply than could be effected in different circumstances. . . . William Craft, the husband, is a dark mulatto, tall, erect and dignified in his appearance, of good mind, good judgment, and every way giving proof of a manly self-reliance and self-respect.

Interest in Ellen was so keen that audience members weren't content only to see her. They asked her questions, and by mid-April she had become so popular that she too spoke during the programs.

The Crafts were open with details of their escape. That was risky. Many runaways kept low profiles, fearing they'd reveal information that could lead slave catchers to them, or that they'd divulge specifics about their route that would make it harder for other slaves to take the same path to freedom. But Ellen wanted their story told in hopes it would reach Macon so her mother would learn that she was safe.

The Fugitive Slave Act

After four months traveling around Massachusetts with the Crafts, Brown left for Europe, ending their first lecture tour. Ellen and William chose to remain in the state and make Boston their home. She quickly got work as a seamstress, but William had no luck finding anyone who would hire a black cabinetmaker. He gave up looking after several weeks and opened a second-hand furniture store. Ellen learned to mend the worn upholstery he sold. But their peaceful existence came crashing down in 1850, with the passage of the harsh Fugitive Slave Act. For the first time, it was illegal for whites, even in the North, to shelter escaped slaves. The punishment for people who assisted runaways was severe: six months in jail and up to a thousand-dollar fine.

The law had a direct impact on the Crafts. Ellen had wanted news of their escape to reach Macon, and it did, with a story in a local newspaper in February 1849. One October day in 1850, John Knight, a white man who'd worked with William in the cabinetmaker's shop, visited William in his store. William was polite but declined Knight's request to show him the sights, and the next day he also declined to visit him in his hotel. William learned that Knight had come to Boston with Willis Hughes, Macon's town jailer. They were there to bring the fugitives back to Georgia.

Boston's antislavery community rallied to their cause. Black men and women guarded William's store against attack; white lawyers used any arguments they could muster to get the two slave hunters arrested—for slandering Ellen, for slandering William, even for smoking and swearing in the streets. This went on for two weeks, until the unwelcome visitors had had enough and left.

But William and Ellen's victory didn't last. The law was against them, as was the president of the United States, Millard Fillmore. He threatened to "call forth the militia" if all other attempts to apprehend the Crafts failed.

With an arrest warrant out, with troops headed to Boston to capture them and with their friends' safety at risk, the Crafts recognized that there was no safe haven in the United States—not even in Massachusetts, their home for two years. They would flee to England, where there was no slavery. First, they married again, this time in a ceremony blessed by their church and the state, and then, on a cold and wet November night, they escaped. Ellen traveled in her own clothing and under her own name, risking capture as she had two years before. They stopped first in Maine, then crossed the border to Canada, which protected fugitive slaves, and finally made the slow voyage across the ocean to Liverpool, England.

In Britain

Activists in Britain had ended slavery in the British West Indies after a long struggle, and they remained tireless fighters, committed to ending slavery in the United States as well. Ellen and William's friends in New England gave them letters of introduction to their counterparts in Britain, but they didn't need one for their old friend William Wells Brown. The fugitive slave from Missouri had been in England for more than a year, and he urged the Georgia fugitives to join him on his lecture tour.

Tour they did, meeting abolitionists, scientists, even nobility. They had a visit from Thomas Dick, an astronomer who took them to his observatory; they spent three days with the journalist and political economist Harriet Martineau; and they met Lady Noel Byron, widow of the poet Lord Byron.

William and Ellen attracted large audiences throughout Britain. William was again the narrator, telling the story of slavery and their courageous escape, but

Ellen was the star attraction. She stood and let everyone see her, but following the English custom, she didn't speak in public. Without saying a word, she kept the audience riveted to their story and turned the spotlight on the injustices faced by American slaves.

Once again, it was Ellen's looks that people talked most about. Her white skin and ladylike behavior took many audience members by surprise. A public that often shared the racial prejudices of American slave owners did not expect a runaway slave to look genteel.

She "is a gentle, refined-looking young creature," an anonymous writer said in an 1853 article, "as fair as most of her British sisters, and in mental qualifications their equal too." A Welsh abolitionist said, "She certainly is a wonderful woman, and interested us more than either of her companions." But some people thought she appeared reserved, reluctant to be in public. A Scottish journalist wrote that after several gentlemen persuaded her to stand, "She was most enthusiastically received. At first she seemed abashed; but the cheering having continued, she courtesied [curtsied] gracefully, and retired."

We may never know how Ellen felt as the crowd applauded—if she was embarrassed at being observed; if she was humble, knowing she was the main attraction; or if her apparent shyness was part of the show, conveying the evils of enslaving women as forcefully as any words. A look, a wave of the hand, a curtsy gave the message: There but for the grace of God go you, your mother, your wife, your sister, your daughter.

Ellen also made an appearance in London in 1851 at the Great Exhibition, a world's fair, where she and William joined other abolitionists, black and white, in a day-long antislavery demonstration. Circulating through the exhibits, each of the blacks took the arm of a white—a man's arm linked with a woman's, a woman's with a man's. The aim, one participant explained, was to show that they regarded the fugitives as their equals "and honored them for their heroic escape from slavery."

Following a summer in London and Bristol, Ellen and William took a two-year break from their public appearances to attend and work at an innovative school in Ockham, a small village outside London. The Ockham School was one of the first vocational schools in Britain, combining classroom instruction with farming and industrial crafts. In the mornings Ellen and William studied reading, writing and mathematics, and in the afternoons William taught carpentry to the boys and Ellen instructed the girls in sewing. Lady Byron helped to fund the school.

In September 1852, the first of their five children was born. The Crafts could have stayed at the Ockham School, where they were offered jobs in the industrial (vocational) department, William as superintendent and Ellen as matron, but instead they moved back to London. With a young child, Ellen no longer participated in the lecture circuit, but she could—and did—speak out forcefully when she needed to.

When rumormongers in the United States circulated a story that Ellen Craft had tired of eking out a living in England and wanted to return to slavery, she fought back. "I have never had the slightest inclination whatever of returning to bondage," she wrote in the *Anti-Slavery Advocate* in 1852:

> God forbid that I should ever be so false to liberty as to prefer slavery in its stead. In fact, since my escape from slavery I have got on much better in every respect than I could have possibly anticipated.... I had much rather starve in England, a free woman, than be a slave for the best man that ever breathed upon the American continent.

She showed the same spirit at a London dinner party, when she confronted the former governor of Jamaica, Edward John Eyre. Governor Eyre had executed George William Gordon, a man accused of inciting black Jamaicans to protest for more land and opportunity. An American newspaper described the encounter on January 18, 1867:

> Ellen knows how to use her tongue with considerable effect, and the ex-Governor was somewhat amazed and embarrassed to hear himself terribly castigated by a lady of whose relation to the negro race he had no idea whatever. Whilst the conversation was going on someone hinted to her that the person to whom she was uttering her indignation was no other than ex-Governor Eyre himself; whereupon, frankly

and unembarrassed, she said, solemnly: "Do not you, yourself, feel now that poor Gordon was most unjustly executed?" The ex-Governor, upon this, was overwhelmed with confusion, turned very red, excused himself and walked to the other end of the room.

Returning to America

The American Civil War, which pitted proslavery Southern forces against the antislavery North, ended in April 1865. Though blacks were now free, Ellen knew they could not be productive citizens without an education. Most couldn't read or write, and those who had worked in the fields didn't know the basics of cooking, cleaning and sewing. Friends in Pennsylvania, Massachusetts and Britain had reached out their hands to help Ellen and William when they escaped slavery, and now she wanted to do the same for the emancipated back home. She dreamed of setting up an institution in Georgia like the Ockham School, where she and William had worked and studied.

In 1869, Ellen and William returned to Boston with three of their children (the other two stayed in England to finish their schooling) and then headed to the South, a place where slavery had ended but racial prejudice was as virulent as ever. Unable to find a farm to buy in Georgia, William purchased one with a partner in South Carolina. Ellen taught black children during the day and adults at night, while William farmed. Their first harvest was good, but any chance for success went up in flames when a band of white men attacked.

Dressed in long white robes and strange conical hats, the masked men, known as the Ku Klux Klan, arrived at night. They torched the barns and other buildings, jeopardizing the children's lives, then burned most of the crops and dashed the Crafts' hopes for success in South Carolina. The aim of the Klan, a violent organization that began in the South at the end of the Civil War and continues to threaten blacks and other minorities even today, was simple and evil: to keep whites in power throughout the South and keep blacks down.

Ellen and William were hindered, but they couldn't be stopped. The couple found another plantation, this time in Georgia, in 1872. There, they farmed, taught and struggled against financial difficulties and prejudice. At one point, they had as many as seventy-five students in their school. But as hard as they worked, the farm never thrived. They could not overcome the antagonism of the whites and the challenges of life in the post–Civil War South. By 1878, they had to close the school.

Still, their black neighbors admired them. "No colored family in the state stands higher in the estimation of the people of Georgia than the Craft family," a black newspaper reported in 1883. Ellen was no longer living on that plantation when she died around 1891, but it is where she asked to be buried.

Born in Georgia as a slave, she was buried in Georgia as a free woman who had spent her life fighting for liberty.

Harriet Tubman

Large groups of fugitives, like this one, successfully escaped from Maryland's Eastern Shore in the late 1850s, generating panic among slaveholders.

CHAPTER 4

"I Was Free, an' They Should Be Free"

Harriet Tubman

WHEN HARRIET TUBMAN WAS ABOUT seven years old, her owner sent her to work for a family on the Eastern Shore of Maryland, not far from where her mother lived. One of her first jobs was to clean the parlor. Her mistress, known as Miss Susan, kept a whip nearby in case she wasn't happy with Harriet's work. "Move those chairs and tables into the middle of the room, sweep the carpet clean, then dust everything, and put them back in their places!" were her mistress's orders to the child.

Harriet moved the furniture, then swept with all her might, sending up clouds of dust. With so much housework to do, she hastily dusted the furniture "so you could see your face in 'em, they shone so," she told an interviewer years later. But when her mistress came into the room, the dust had settled onto the furniture once again. "What do you mean by doing my work this way, you—" she scolded. Though Harriet protested that she had done what she was told, Miss Susan let her whip fly, striking Harriet over and over on head, face and neck until the mistress's sister Emily entered the room, unable to bear the child's cries. Chasing Miss Susan away, Emily patiently told Harriet always to wait until the dust settled before wiping the furniture clean.

Harriet never forgot that beating or the other cruelties she suffered as a slave. When she was an adult, she said, "Slavery was the next thing to hell." By then, she had fled from bondage in Maryland, only to return several times to lead relatives, friends and others—about seventy people in all—out of slavery. Though her married name was Harriet Tubman, many Americans called her Moses, after the man who led the Hebrews from slavery to freedom in the Bible.

The biblical name was fitting because Tubman believed God had chosen her for the job. "I could hear the Lord," she explained. "'It's you I want, Harriet Tubman,'—just as clear as I heard him speak—an' then I'd go again down South an' bring up my brothers an' sisters." Tubman was a guide on the Underground Railroad, the abolitionist network that led fugitive slaves to freedom in the Northern United States and Canada.

Early Years

Harriet Tubman was born Araminta Ross sometime between 1820 and 1822 to Ben Ross and Harriet "Rit" Green. Her parents were slaves on Maryland's Eastern Shore. They weren't officially married—slaves were not allowed to marry legally—but they lived as husband and wife, though they were often apart, serving two different masters. Harriet was one of nine children. Many of her childhood memories were bitter; she saw two of her sisters sold away from the family into slavery in the Deep South. In later years, Harriet described to a biographer the profound impression this violent separation made on her: She never closed her eyes without seeing the horsemen coming and hearing the screams of women and children, "as they were being dragged away to a far worse slavery than that they were enduring there."

But she had happy memories too, and she forged deep attachments to her family, which drove her to risk life and freedom to free relatives and friends. Even as a child of four or five, she enjoyed caring for her younger siblings. While her mother worked in the master's kitchen, Harriet took care of the baby and her little brother. "I used to be in a hurry for her to go, so's I could play the baby was a pig in a bag, an' hold him up by the bottom of his dress," she later recalled. "I had a nice frolic with that baby, swingin' him all round, his feet in the dress an' his little head an' arms touchin' the floor, 'cause I was too small to hold him higher."

Though slavery along the Eastern Shore was generally less brutal than plantation slavery in the Deep South, slaves were worked hard from an early age. When Harriet was about six or seven, her owner placed her with another family, who made her check muskrat traps in the cold water of a marsh, even when she was sick with the measles.

Punishment was a part of life, and though she feared the whip, she was a child and sometimes took chances. Once, she watched her master and mistress quarreling and noticed a sugar bowl nearby.

> An' that sugar, right by me, did look so nice, an' my Missus's back was turned to me while she was fightin' with her husband, so I just put my fingers in the sugar bowl to take one lump an' maybe she heard me an' she turned an' saw me. The next minute she had the raw hide down; I give one jump out of the door, an' I saw they came after me, but I just flew an' they didn't catch me. I run, an' run, an' I run. I passed many a house, but I didn't dare to stop, for they all knew my Missus an' they would send me back.

Harriet hid in a pigpen at a nearby farm for five days, competing with "an old sow an' perhaps eight or ten little pigs" for the food. Hungry and with no place else to go, she finally went back to her master's home, where she was welcomed with a whipping.

Harriet's life changed when she was a teenager and was made to work on a farmer's fields. One night she was standing at the door of a dry goods store while a slave from a nearby farm was being pursued by his overseer. As the fleeing man approached the entrance, the overseer shouted at Harriet and others to tie him up; she refused, so the overseer picked up a heavy weight and flung it at the man. It missed him, hitting Harriet instead. It broke her skull and sliced off a piece of a shawl she was wearing, driving it into her head. "They carried me to the house all bleedin' an' faintin'. I had no bed, no place to lie down on at all, an' they lay me on the seat of the loom, an' I stayed there all that day an' next." Despite her injury, Harriet was soon sent back into the field. "[A]n' there I worked with the blood an' sweat rollin' down my face until I couldn't see," she remembered.

Her brain was permanently injured. For the rest of her life, she would unpredictably drop off to sleep—sometimes in the course of a conversation or the middle of a task. Even while leading runaways to freedom, Tubman sometimes fell asleep by the side of the road—though, she said proudly, she "never lost a passenger" on the Underground Railroad.

After the brain injury, Tubman began to have some unusual symptoms. At times she had sensations of leaving her body to fly over fields and towns like a bird and of hearing "such music as filled all the air." She understood these feelings to be religious experiences and often spoke to God directly, certain that he heard her voice and answered her.

Some time after her injury, Tubman was hired out to a shipyard owner. As she pulled canal boats and cut logs in the woods, she discovered a secret network of blacks, slave and free, who helped runaways escape. With more freedom of movement than blacks in towns or on farms, these laborers directed fugitives to safe houses and pointed out the safest routes to travel. In years to come, this network would help Tubman carry out her own rescues.

Around this time, Harriet met and married a free black, John Tubman. Free blacks like John could legally marry, though any children they had would be slaves if the mother was a slave. Hoping to buy her freedom, Harriet worked hard to earn extra money beyond the fixed sum she owed her master each year. When her owner died in 1849, his widow advertised a sale of slaves. Knowing she would be sold to work on the cotton or rice fields in the Deep South, Harriet Tubman made up her mind to flee, though John would stay behind in Maryland. The first time she ran off, it was with her brothers, but they became fearful and dragged her back home with them. On the Monday after their return, she got word that she would definitely be sold that night. This time, she decided to go alone.

Traveling the Underground Railroad

Tubman was afraid to tell her mother to her face that she was leaving, for fear that Rit's loud cries would betray her plans. So on the evening of her escape, she approached the house where her mother worked, singing a song with a message she hoped Rit would understand:

> *I'm sorry I'm goin' to leave you,*
> *Farewell, oh farewell;*
> *But I'll meet you in the mornin',*
> *Farewell, oh farewell.*

I'll meet you in the mornin',
I'm bound for the Promised Land,
On the other side of Jordan,
Bound for the Promised Land.

In the years that followed, people who met Tubman often commented on her beautiful voice. She would make good use of it in the songs she sang to deliver coded messages to runaways and to embellish the stories she told about her past. Tubman fled on foot as far as she could run that night—to a safe house whose owner smuggled her in his wagon to the next stop on the Underground Railroad. She continued her flight, always at night, guided by the North Star and sympathetic people, until she arrived in the free state of Pennsylvania. "When I found I had crossed that line," she later reported, "I looked at my hands to see if I was the same person. There was such a glory over everythin'; the sun came like gold through the trees, an' over the fields, an' I felt like I was in Heaven."

Tubman's joy at her own freedom was tinged with sadness, however, since she had left her family behind. She recalled:

I was free; but there was no one to welcome me to the land of freedom. I was a stranger in a strange land; an' my home, after all, was down in Maryland; because my father, my mother, my brothers, an' sisters, an' friends were there. But I was free, an' they should be free. I would make a home in the North an' bring them there, God helpin' me.

From the earliest days of American history slaves had run away from their owners, but as the slavery debate heated up, more and more people began to help them. The term *Underground Railroad* didn't come into use in the United States until the 1830s, when steam railways were built. This antislavery network borrowed many words from the railroads: "conductors" hid slaves (their "passengers") in their wagons or guided them to "stations" (barns and safe houses), where "stationmasters" received them.

Many slaves escaped, but few did what Tubman did: risk being recaptured by returning to free others. Tubman believed God had selected her to free her people, however, and would protect her as she led them to freedom. Thomas Garrett, the white Underground Railroad stationmaster in Wilmington, Delaware, said he had "never met with any person, of any color, who had more confidence in the voice of God, as spoken direct to her soul."

At first Tubman was cautious, going only as far as Baltimore, where she would not be recognized, to bring her niece Kessiah to Philadelphia, and a few months later to retrieve her brother Moses and two other runaways. By the fall of 1851, however, Tubman had returned to Maryland's Eastern Shore, where she was known and in danger of being captured, to bring out her husband. To her surprise and anger, he had taken up with another woman. She decided that if he could do without her, she could do without him, and conducted another group of slaves to Philadelphia instead.

When the Fugitive Slave Act was passed in 1850, runaways were at greater risk even in the Northern states, where slave catchers actively hunted them down. It became safer for slaves to leave the country altogether, and Tubman led many from Pennsylvania through New York and on to St. Catharines, in Canada. Over the course of the next decade, she made at least a dozen more trips, freeing about sixty more people. She also gave detailed instructions on escape routes to about another fifty people.

Tubman skillfully negotiated the challenges of these trips. She had to guide her passengers through the countryside and often had to pass time waiting for them in villages where she might be recognized. She became an expert mimic. She would wear a silk dress to impersonate a middle-class free black woman. Bent over, her head covered in a sunbonnet, she appeared to be a feeble old lady. Returning from the market one day with two live fowl in hand, she caught sight of her old master on the street. Tubman immediately pulled at the string holding the legs of her chickens together, causing them to squawk so loudly that he looked at the birds instead of her.

She always led her fugitives out on Saturday nights; no newspapers were published on Sundays, so she had a day's lead before runaway notices could be posted. If she had to leave her fugitives while scouting the territory, she warned them of trouble by singing spirituals with coded clues. Tubman later explained, "If I sing: 'Moses, go down in Egypt, / Till ole Pharo' let me go; Hadn't been for

Adam's fall / Shouldn't hab to died at all,' then they don't come out, for there's danger in the way."

She carried a pistol for protection, and sometimes had to point it at runaways who lost their nerve and wanted to go back. "Go on or die," she would tell them. Tubman could not risk having a fugitive captured and revealing everyone else's location.

Anyone suspected of helping slaves escape was watched closely, but Tubman had a knack for keeping her exploits secret and knowing who could be trusted. When she got word that her brothers Ben, Robert and Henry were to be sold at Christmastime in 1854, she dictated a letter in coded language to Jacob Jackson, a free black back in Maryland. (Tubman couldn't read or write.) "Read my letter to the old folks, and give my love to them," she said, "and tell my brothers to be always watching unto prayer, and when the good old ship of Zion comes along, to be ready to step aboard." Tubman herself was "the good old ship of Zion," and she was telling her brothers to be ready to run off with her.

Free blacks were often suspected of helping slaves escape, so the postal workers were reading Jackson's mail. When they couldn't figure the letter out, they called him in. Jackson played his part well, flinging the letter away with the words "That letter can't be meant for me, no how. I can't make head nor tail of it." He promptly alerted Tubman's brothers to be ready to leave at a moment's notice.

Their flight wasn't easy. Robert's wife, Mary, was in labor with their third child, but if he stayed behind he would be sold, with no chance of ever seeing her or their children again. It was just as hard for Tubman. She caught a glimpse of her mother, whom she hadn't seen for five years, through the window of her cottage, but she knew that her mother would cry out if she saw her, putting all of them in danger. Their father, Ben, knew that they were there and that he would be grilled by the authorities after his sons' escape. Vowing not to *see* them, he tied a handkerchief over his eyes and accompanied them as they set off.

When Ben's former master was questioned by slave catchers, he recounted what Ben and Rit had told him. "Old Rit says not one of 'em came this Christmas. She was looking for 'em most all day, and most broke her heart about it," the master said. "Old Ben says that he hasn't seen one of his children this Christmas." The slave catchers trusted Ben's word.

Over the next six years, Tubman repeatedly returned to Maryland. Time and again, she tried to free her sister Rachel, but Rachel refused to leave without her children. She came for all of them in late 1860, but Rachel had died and the children were nowhere to be found.

Between trips, Tubman would fund-raise or do odd jobs to earn money for her next rescue. She also asked the abolitionist community for financial help. Thomas Garrett, the Underground Railroad stationmaster from Delaware, told her story to sympathetic antislavery friends in England, who sent money for her. She once sat on the floor of the New York City Anti-Slavery Office, refusing to budge until they came up with the funds she needed to move her parents to a free state. She dropped off to sleep and awoke to find the money she needed waiting for her.

Harriet's father helped to arrange one of Tubman's rescues. Joe Bailey was a highly skilled timber worker owned by William Hughlett, a lumber merchant notorious for his brutality to his slaves. Joe secretly approached Ben one evening, asking him to alert Harriet that he and his brother Bill were anxious to escape. Tubman arrived in the area a week or two later, hoping to lead her sister to freedom. When this proved impossible, she set out instead with Joe, Bill and two more slaves. Hughlett was determined to reclaim his property, posting a princely reward for the capture of Joe, his most valuable slave.

The money was a powerful inducement to slave catchers to pursue the runaways without letup, and it took the fugitives two weeks to get to Wilmington, Delaware—normally a two-day trip. Once, while they hid in a hole where farmers stored potatoes, their pursuers passed only a few feet away. In Delaware, abolitionist Thomas Garrett helped arrange the slaves' escape over a closely watched bridge into Pennsylvania. He found a pair of black bricklayers who were willing to hide the runaways in a secret compartment in their wagon, beneath a pile of bricks. The bricklayers then cleverly distracted the slave catchers' attention by singing loudly as they drove their wagon over the river to freedom.

Though by this time both of Tubman's parents were free, they were still living in Maryland, and authorities correctly suspected that Ben was helping slaves get away. Tubman was afraid he would be arrested, so in May 1857 she came down to help her parents leave. In their seventies, they couldn't walk like the young runaways, so Tubman improvised a kind of buggy out of a pair of old wagon wheels with a board as a seat, pulled by an old horse with a straw collar, to carry her parents to Wilmington. From there they went to the antislavery headquarters in Philadelphia, then on to New York City and Rochester, New York, and finally to St. Catharines, to join their sons, grandchildren and great-grandchildren.

Returning to Maryland that summer, Tubman helped a group of thirty-nine slaves make plans to escape, though she did not accompany them. The flight of large numbers of slaves in the fall of 1857 ignited a wave of panic among slaveholders, who held public meetings and published articles claiming, illogically, that blacks (who were running away in increasing numbers) were happy as slaves. Slave owners sent out more patrols to track down fugitives, so it was no longer safe for Tubman to remain in Maryland to help other escapees. She returned to her family and the runaway community in Canada to help her parents and organize aid for the poorest fugitives.

John Brown

In Canada, Tubman met the renowned antislavery militant John Brown, who stood out from the other abolitionists she knew because of his support for violent tactics. He and his sons had taken up arms against proslavery settlers in Kansas a few years before, and by 1858 he was planning a raid on a federal armory in Harpers Ferry, Virginia, hoping to ignite a slave rebellion that would end slavery in America.

The militant and the ex-slave made a profound impression on each other. To Brown, Tubman was someone who could guide his fighters through the wilderness of Virginia and inspire fugitive slaves to join his rebellion. He called her "one of the best and bravest persons on this continent" and "*General* Tubman."

But though Tubman did recruit men for his rebellion, in the end none of the Canadian fugitives she lined up went south to join his forces. And though he was counting on her help at the Harpers Ferry raid, she was not around at the time. Historical records are hazy about the reason. She may have been ill, but it is also possible that she kept her distance, knowing that Brown's plan was bound to fail.

Later, she praised his legacy. "When I think how he gave up his life for our people, an' how he never flinched, but was so brave to the end, it's clear to me it wasn't mortal man, it was God in him," she said. "He done more in dyin' than one hundred men would in livin'.""

In New York

Tubman soon moved her parents, who were unhappy in Canada, back to the United States. Her friend and admirer William H. Seward, an antislavery senator, sold her a house and piece of land in Auburn, New York, very cheaply. To raise money to support her parents, she told the story of her life as a slave and conductor on the Underground Railroad to abolitionist conventions and parlor meetings, where collections were taken for her benefit. One person who heard her wrote, "She has great dramatic power; the scene rises before you as she saw it, and her voice and language change with her different actors."

In the spring of 1860, Tubman traveled from Auburn to Boston to attend an antislavery conference, stopping along the way in Troy, New York. She soon learned that Charles Nalle, a man who had escaped from slavery in Virginia two years before, had been recaptured. A crowd of pro- and antislavery people, black and white, had gathered at the government office where he was being held. Disguised as a bent old woman in shawl and sunbonnet, Tubman made her way up to the second story of the building. As she remembered the event years later, people in the crowd recognized her and said, "There stands Moses yet, an' as long as she is there, he is safe."

As the sheriff and his deputies began to escort Nalle from the building to the office of the judge who would hear the case, Tubman made her move. Knowing that the waiting crowd of black people would provide the backup she needed, she gave a signal to surge forward, while she attempted to free Nalle from the grip of the officers. Down the stairs she moved with Nalle in her arms, and whenever the officers laid hold of the fugitive, the crowd pulled him back. "Drag us out! Drag him to the river! Drown him, but don't let them have him!" cried Tubman, and the crowd held on, conveying Nalle and Tubman to the river, where a small boat was waiting to ferry Nalle across to the other side.

Alerted by telegraph that Nalle was on his way, the police on the far side of the river captured him. But Tubman and the crowd crossed the river by ferry and made their way toward the judge's chambers, where Nalle was being held. Shots were fired, stones were flung, and a strong black man named Martin forced open the judge's door, only to be knocked unconscious by an ax-wielding officer waiting at the entrance. When Tubman told the story later, she said she flung Nalle "across my shoulder like a bag of meal." As shots continued to be fired, she and others commandeered a passing farmer's wagon to take Nalle, now bleeding from the shackles on his wrists and wearing Harriet's bonnet, to a safe house in the countryside, where he hid until abolitionists managed to purchase his freedom.

Civil War

The American Civil War began on April 12, 1861, when shots were fired at Fort Sumter, South Carolina. For President Abraham Lincoln, this was a war to preserve the Union, not to end slavery. But to Harriet Tubman, the Union could not win this war until Lincoln set the slaves free. She insisted:

> They may send the flower of their young men down South. . . . They may send them one year, two years, three years, till they are *tired* of sendin', or till they use up all the young men. All no use! God's ahead of Master Lincoln. God won't let Master Lincoln beat the South till he does *the right thing*. Master Lincoln, he's a great man, an' I am a poor Negro; but the Negro can tell Master Lincoln how to save the money an' the young men. He can do it by settin' the Negroes free.

Tubman's abolitionist contacts introduced her to Governor John Andrew of Massachusetts, and in January 1862 he arranged for her to get to South Carolina. He knew of her reputation for traveling undetected and thought she could put her skills to use as a scout for the Union army. Tubman found other ways to make herself useful as well—as nurse, trainer of freed slaves, spy, recruiter of black troops and even military adviser.

At the Sea Islands, off the coast of South Carolina, which the Union had succeeded in capturing, Tubman set up a washhouse and taught freed black women to launder, sew and bake for Union soldiers so they could earn money rather than take handouts from the government. Tubman had ways of ferreting out information about enemy encampments and fortifications. As one visitor to the Union camp reported, "She has made it a business to see all contrabands [slaves who had crossed over to the Union lines] escaping from the rebels, and is able to get more intelligence than anybody else." This intelligence was valuable to the Union forces, most famously on June 1, 1863, when Tubman helped guide Colonel James Montgomery and his black troops on an expedition up the Combahee River to destroy the enemy's supply line and clear underwater mines. Moving upriver on three gunboats, the troops burned plantations, confiscated their supplies of rice and cotton, and alerted the slaves that they had arrived to ferry them to freedom.

Frantically, the slaves gathered their children and whatever else they could to get to the gunboats. Tubman saw mothers grabbing pots of rice right off the fire, putting the pots on their heads and lifting children on their shoulders. Balancing pot and child, women rushed to the boats with a "young one hangin' on behind," Tubman said, "one hand round the mother's forehead to hold on, the other hand diggin' into the rice pot, eatin' with all its might." And it wasn't just mothers and children. "Some had bags on their backs with pigs in them; some had chickens tied by the legs. An' so child squallin', chickens squawkin', an' pigs squealin' they all come runnin' to the gunboats . . . [like] the children of Israel, comin' out of Egypt."

Desperate to be free, these slaves hung on to the overloaded rowboats that would shuttle them to the gunboats and away from their plantations. The captain called on Tubman for help: "Moses, come here and speak to your people," he shouted. Unsure how to command them, because "they didn't know anythin' about me an' I didn't know what to say," Tubman did what she had done when she herself had run from slavery—she sang:

> *Come from the east;*
> *Come from the west;*
> *'Mong all the glorious nations*
> *This glorious one's the best;*
> *Come 'long, come 'long!*
> *Don't be alarmed,*

For Uncle Sam is rich enough
To give you all a farm.

At that, they threw up their hands and shouted, "Glory!", freeing the row-boats to push off.

The Combahee River raid liberated hundreds of slaves. Tubman was proud of what they had done, and in a letter she dictated a month later, she declared:

Don't you think we colored people are entitled to some of the credit for that exploit, under the lead of the brave Colonel Montgomery? We weakened the rebels somewhat on the Combahee River, by taking and bringing away *seven hundred and fifty-six* [freed slaves] ... and this, too, without the loss of a single life on our part, though we had good reason to believe that a number of rebels bit the dust.

Tubman claimed that she herself delivered nearly a hundred of the men to the Union army as new recruits and was now "trying to find places for those able to work ... so as to lighten the burden on the government as much as possible, while at the same time they learn to respect themselves by earning their own living."

A month and a half later, Tubman was called up to Fort Wagner at Charleston Harbor, where the black troops of the 54th Massachusetts Infantry Regiment fought bravely, with high casualties. Tubman later described how she nursed the wounded:

I'd go to the hospital, I would, early every mornin'. I'd get a big chunk of ice, I would, an' put it in a basin, an' fill it with water; then I'd take a sponge an' begin. First man I'd come to, I'd thrash away the flies, an' they'd rise, they would, like bees round a hive. Then I'd begin to bathe their wounds, an' by the time I'd bathed off three or four, the fire an' heat would have melted the ice an' made the water warm, an' it would be as red as clear blood. Then I'd go an' get more ice, I would, an' by the time I got to the next ones, the flies would be round the first ones, black an' thick as ever.

Later in the war, a Union surgeon called Tubman to Fernandina, Florida, where soldiers were dying of dysentery, an infection that causes severe diarrhea. "I dug some roots an' herbs an' made a tea for the doctor [who was himself suffering from the ailment] an' the disease stopped on him," she later told a friend. The doctor told her to give it to the soldiers. "So I boiled up a great boiler of roots an' herbs, an' the general told a man to take two cans an' go round an' give it to all in the camp that needed it, an' it cured them."

After the War

Like many freed slaves, Tubman came face to face with racial prejudice in the North after the war. On the train she took home from Philadelphia to New York, the conductor did not want to honor the half-fare ticket she carried as a government worker. "Come, hustle out of here! We don't carry niggers for half fare," she later reported him saying. When Tubman refused to move, the conductor and two other men tossed her into the baggage car, breaking her arm and a few ribs.

Tubman arrived home in pain, exhausted and almost penniless, but her struggle wasn't over. She now embarked on a frustrating uphill battle to win a government pension for her army service. She had served unofficially and virtually unpaid for over three years, but she had no documents to prove it. Over the next three decades, she submitted letters from influential people confirming her upstanding character and her wartime service as a nurse and scout. Henry K. Durant, an assistant army surgeon, wrote that he had "frequent and ample opportunities to observe her general deportment; particularly her kindness and attention to the sick and suffering of her own race." Nevertheless, it wasn't until she was in her seventies, more than thirty years after the war, that she received a small pension.

During her first winter home after the war, unable to work because of her injury on the train, Tubman was forced to burn the rails of the fence around her property for heat. When the cupboard was bare, she depended on money donated by friends—particularly old friends from the abolition movement. Yet despite her poverty, Tubman never turned anyone away. One of her friends described her household this way: "The aged, ... the babe deserted, the demented, the epileptic, the blind, the paralyzed, the consumptive all have found shelter and welcome. At no time can I recall the little home to have sheltered less than six or eight wrecks of humanity entirely dependent upon Harriet for their all."

Tubman became involved in women's causes but never forgot the needs of her own people. At the founding meeting of the National Association of Colored Women in Washington, DC, in 1896, she was introduced as "Mother Tubman," the oldest activist there. She spoke to her audience about the need for "homes for our aged ones" and collected money for one that she had been planning to build in Auburn for years. Many former slaves had lost contact with their families when they came North; now they lived alone and were excluded from white old age homes. Tubman bought the land for her shelter, and in 1908 the Harriet Tubman Home for Aged and Infirm Negroes opened, with financial support from her church.

She also supported the woman suffrage movement, the cause to give women the right to vote, and was enthusiastically applauded at a women's rights convention in Rochester, New York, as the "great black liberator."

Near the end of Tubman's life, local and national newspapers ran occasional articles reminding people of her achievements—sometimes even inflating them; one writer likened her to Joan of Arc, and the *Sun* newspaper in New York called her the "founder of the Underground Railroad." When she died of pneumonia in 1913, several hundred citizens of Auburn, including many dignitaries, attended her funeral, where speakers evoked her righteous and heroic life.

The Auburn community, black and white, erected a bronze memorial on the courthouse building a year later. The plaque praised the woman who "BRAVED EVERY DANGER AND OVERCAME EVERY OBSTACLE," and ended with the words that Tubman herself had used to sum up her greatest achievement. Though transcribed in the dialect that white people of the time often used to demean African-Americans, the words also reflected the entire community's admiration for her: "ON MY UNDERGROUND RAILROAD I NEBBER RUN MY TRAIN OFF DE TRACK AND I NEBBER LOS' A PASSENGER."

For decades after Tubman's death, it was African-Americans who kept her memory alive, telling her story to students in segregated schools. It took 1960s civil rights activists to insist that all Americans needed to know about black heroes. Biographies of Harriet Tubman, mostly for children and young adults, began to appear, and today, there are well over fifty children's books about Tubman still in print. In 1978, the U.S. Postal Service issued a Harriet Tubman stamp—the first stamp honoring a black American woman. Eight years later, a survey of American eleventh-graders showed that more students knew Harriet Tubman had been a conductor on the Underground Railroad than could name a general in the American Revolution, even though one of those was George Washington.

Drawn by Harry Townsend

"'SO YOU'RE THE LITTLE WOMAN WHO WROTE THE BOOK THAT MADE THIS GREAT WAR!'"

604

Harriet Beecher Stowe met President Abraham Lincoln at the White House in December 1862, hoping to convince him to free America's slaves.

This illustration of *Uncle Tom's Cabin* shows gentle Eva befriending the little slave girl, Topsy, with the words "I love you because you haven't any Father, or Mother, or Friends."

EVA AND TOPSY.

CHAPTER 5

"I Will Write Something. I Will If I Live"

Harriet Beecher Stowe

A STORY WAS PASSED DOWN in the family of the American author Harriet Beecher Stowe. It tells us that Stowe visited President Abraham Lincoln in the White House on a damp, chilly December day in 1862, in the midst of the American Civil War and just weeks before he was to free the slaves in the Confederate states. The president greeted Stowe with a startling declaration. "So," he announced, "you're the little woman who wrote the book that made this great war!"

If Lincoln was exaggerating, it wasn't by much. Ten years earlier, Stowe had published *Uncle Tom's Cabin; or, Life among the Lowly*. The book told the story of slavery—of children sold away from their parents, of husbands and wives separated forever, of slaves toiling long hours in cotton fields and getting beaten when they displeased their masters. By painting a picture of slavery that many Americans had never seen before, the book turned the hearts of Northerners against slavery, infuriated Southerners and changed American history.

Uncle Tom's Cabin, originally released in installments in the magazine *National Era*, was an instant success. One reader wrote, "Weekly, as the *Era* arrives, our family, consisting of twelve individuals, is called together to listen to the reading of 'Uncle Tom's Cabin.'" When it was published as a book in March 1852, the novel sold ten thousand copies in the first seven days and three hundred thousand in the first year. By the end of 1852, three hundred babies in Boston had been named Eva, after one of the most sympathetic characters in the novel. It was the time of the gold rush, and 3,000 miles (4,800 kilometers) away in California, where it was not easy to lay hands on a copy of the book, miners shared the book around at twenty-five cents a turn.

Keeping up with demand became a difficult chore. A month after the book came out, the publisher announced, "Three paper mills are constantly at work manufacturing the paper, and three power presses are working twenty-four hours per day, in printing it, and more than one hundred book-binders are incessantly plying their trade to bind them, and still it has been impossible, as yet, to supply the demand." Overseas, the sales were even higher. In England, Stowe's book sold a million and a half copies in the year after publication, and by the start of the American Civil War, the book had been translated into sixteen languages.

The Story of *Uncle Tom's Cabin*

Uncle Tom's Cabin opens on the veranda of a Kentucky home, where two men are drinking wine. Mr. Shelby is knee-deep in debt to his guest, the slave trader Haley. To discharge his debts, Shelby reluctantly agrees to sell Haley his most dependable slave, Tom, "an uncommon fellow . . . steady, honest, capable, manages my whole farm like a clock." Haley also offers to buy the beautiful Eliza, Mrs. Shelby's personal servant, but Shelby insists his wife would never part with her. He agrees, however, to sell Harry, Eliza's little boy.

Eliza overhears this conversation and resolves to escape with Harry to Canada, where she believes her husband has fled. In the most famous scene in the novel, Eliza crosses the ice-covered Ohio River clutching little Harry tightly in her arms and leaping from ice floe to ice floe with "wild cries and desperate energy." She scrambles up the bank on the Ohio side of the river and finds shelter with sympathetic white people.

Meanwhile, sold away from his family, Tom is on a riverboat when little Evangeline St. Clare, returning with her father to their opulent home in New Orleans, falls overboard. Tom plunges into the river to save Eva. A bond develops between him and the child, who asks her grateful father to buy the slave for her.

Eva's father is an indulgent master who knows all too well that slavery is wrong; he calls it "the essence of all abuse." As a spoiled and lazy Southern gentleman, however, he has no idea how to live without a household full of slaves. This troubles young Eva. "I feel sad for our poor people," she says. "I wish, papa, they were all free." (One of the slaves Eva feels sorry for—Topsy, a child as mischievous as Eva is angelic—became one of the book's most popular characters. Only Eva touches Topsy's heart, helping her turn from her "wicked" ways.)

But Eva is in failing health, and as she slowly fades she becomes increasingly attached to Tom. The two share a deep Christian faith that death is only the beginning of life in heaven, and in Eva's last days, Tom carries her under the orange trees and sings hymns to her. Then one night, as "a glorious smile passed over her face," Eva dies.

In gratitude for Tom's devotion to his daughter, St. Clare has promised to free him to return to his family. But Tom's emancipation papers are not complete when tragedy strikes: St. Clare is killed breaking up a brawl. His unfeeling wife, Marie, who believes that "some were born to rule and some to serve," refuses to free Tom and sells off all the St. Clare slaves.

After a grueling journey, Tom arrives at the cotton plantation of the sadistic Simon Legree, who soon sees in Tom a powerful worker who can serve him as a slave driver, a slave who oversees other slaves. But Tom steadfastly refuses to become Legree's brutal enforcer, igniting a smoldering resentment in his master.

Tom's story ends tragically when Legree beats him to death. But Stowe doesn't close her book on this bleak note. Eliza arrives safely in Canada, where she finds her husband. Safe in the North as well, Topsy trains to become a Christian missionary. The Shelbys' oldest son returns to the farm after his father's death, freeing the family's slaves, who agree to stay on to work—this time for wages.

Popularity of the Book

Uncle Tom's Cabin was a page-turner, gripping readers with its fast-moving plot, emotional scenes and strong Christian message. As the novel's popularity soared, America's nineteenth-century marketers devised endless spin-offs. You could buy plates painted with Tom and Eva, china statuettes of Eliza and Harry, and Eva and Topsy paper dolls. You could even play an "Uncle Tom and Little Eva" card game. People flocked to halls, where they could view panoramas—giant multilayered paintings of scenes from the book.

Eliza's dramatic escape in particular inspired sentimental poets and songwriters, who wrote verses like these:

> *Like a fawn from the arrow, startled and wild,*
> *A woman swept by us, bearing a child;*
> *In her eye was the night of a settled despair,*
> *And her brow was o'ershaded with anguish and care.*

By far the most important spin-offs were the Tom plays. In Stowe's time, authors didn't hold a broadly defined copyright on their work, so anyone could take another writer's story and turn it into a play, and the stage version didn't have to be true to the original. In fact, the first Tom play, mounted in Baltimore, was proslavery. One of the most successful antislavery productions was staged in Troy, New York. Its directions for the closing scene were designed to leave no one in the audience with dry eyes:

> Gorgeous clouds, tinted with sunlight. Eva, robed in white, is discovered on the back of a milk-white dove, with expanded wings, as if just soaring upward. Her hands are extended in benediction over St. Clare and Uncle Tom, who are kneeling and gazing up to her. Impressive music—slow curtain.

People clamored to get seats. One letter writer complained to the *New-York Daily Tribune* that there was so much pushing that a young lady in his party "was carried by the crowd more than twenty yards [eighteen meters] on the opening of the doors, during which her feet did not touch the floor, and 'landed' in a remote part of the house."

With the book and its offshoots everywhere, arguments about slavery now became arguments about *Uncle Tom's Cabin* too. Nothing Northern abolitionists did had ever stung Southern pride quite like this book, and Southerners fought back. Within three years of *Uncle Tom's* publication, fourteen anti-Tom novels came out to counter Stowe's picture of slave life. *Uncle Robin, in His Cabin in Virginia, and Tom without One in Boston* was just one of the books to claim that slaves were better off protected by humane masters than left to their own devices. Southern theater producers, meanwhile, capitalized on the popularity of the book but reversed its message. In New Orleans, *Uncle Tom's Cabin: or, Life at the South as It Is* places Tom in Canada, shivering in the cold and longing to return to his plantation.

Stowe's opponents were also quick to argue that she had never lived in the South, and they were right. Stowe had visited Kentucky, though for only a short time. But she'd met with and talked to freed slaves in Cincinnati, Ohio, where she once lived. From her cook, Eliza Buck, she had learned how powerless slaves were. In a letter, Stowe wrote that Buck had "often told me how without any warning, she was suddenly forced into a carriage, & saw her little mistress screaming & stretching her arms from the window towards her, as she was driven away."

To answer her critics, Stowe supplied proof of the book's accuracy. Her five-hundred-page *Key to Uncle Tom's Cabin*, published in 1853, sold one hundred thousand copies within a year. It told her readers, for example, that the loyal Uncle Tom was based in part on Josiah Henson, who, like Tom, was deeply religious and managed his owner's plantation. Henson published his autobiography in 1849.

Early Life

Harriet Beecher was born in 1811 in Litchfield, Connecticut. Her mother, Roxana Foote Beecher, was a cultured woman, fluent in French and passionate about novels and poetry. Her father, a Presbyterian minister named Lyman Beecher, was altogether different. In his opinion, novels were "trash," not an unusual view for a churchman of that time. Beecher was one of the most important evangelical preachers of his day. Although virtually everyone in America was Christian then, evangelical preachers felt they were on a mission to wipe out America's sins (like drunkenness and dueling), revive people's faith and transform the nation into a perfect Christian republic.

Though her father's religion was severe, it didn't stifle his children. With older brothers and a father who enjoyed the outdoors, Harriet was exposed to lots of action. She went out with the boys to collect walnuts and chestnuts, and even remembered "putting on a little black coat which I thought looked more like the boys', casting needle and thread to the wind, and working almost like one possessed for a day and a half, till in the afternoon the wood was all in and piled, and the chips swept up."

Lyman also made sure that Harriet had a well-rounded education. At age eight, she was sent to the Litchfield Female Academy, which normally didn't admit girls until they were twelve. In those days, memory work was important, and by the time she started school, Harriet had already learned twenty-seven hymns and two chapters of the Bible by heart. This special school also offered girls subjects normally restricted to boys, like higher mathematics.

Her favorite teacher ignited an interest in writing, and at age nine Harriet volunteered to write a composition a week. It's hard to imagine a nine-year-old today tackling the topic "Can the immortality of the soul be proved by the light of nature?" But growing up in a religious home, Harriet understood the question (which meant, *Can we prove scientifically that people's souls live on after they die?*).

At age thirteen, she moved on to the Hartford Female Seminary, a school started by her older sister, Catharine, who believed that women could learn more than painting fans and a bit of music, two typical subjects for girls at that time. Catharine's young women studied what young men did, including Latin and science. They also published their own newspaper, the *School Gazette*, which Harriet helped edit.

After she graduated at age sixteen, Harriet returned to the school and taught composition for five years. She also began to discover what kind of writing she most liked to do. To her brother George, she explained, "[I]t is as much my vocation to preach on paper as it is that of my brothers to preach viva voce [out loud]."

It would take a while, but preaching on paper is how she would eventually make her mark.

In Cincinnati

In 1832 the family moved west to Cincinnati, where her father had been invited to head a new religious college. Her sister Catharine opened a new school, but Harriet begged off teaching so she could throw herself into her writing. She joined a writers' group whose name, the Semi-Colon Club, offered no clue to her future talents, since Harriet never learned to punctuate correctly. (Years later, she wrote to a friend, "My printers always inform me that I know nothing of punctuation, & I give thanks that I have no responsibility for any of its absurdities.") The reactions of her fellow writers to her stories helped Harriet develop the intimate style that became her trademark. She wrote as though she were a guest in your living room engaging you in friendly conversation. As she began to polish her style, she also made good use of her keen ear for American dialects, which helped bring characters to life.

Though Harriet was finding much to enjoy in Cincinnati in the 1830s, her country was less happy. The slavery debate was pitting American against American. The Beechers were all opposed to slavery, but they didn't agree on how to end it. Harriet's father occasionally preached against it, but he wanted freed blacks deported to the American colony of Liberia, in Africa. Catharine also opposed slavery, but she criticized radical women abolitionists who dared speak out in public. Harriet's brother Edward, a minister, became an outspoken abolitionist after his friend Elijah Lovejoy, editor of an antislavery newspaper, was murdered by a mob in 1837. Her brother Henry Ward Beecher, the most famous preacher of his time, would later raise money from his pulpit in Brooklyn, New York, to buy slaves their freedom, and even to purchase rifles, popularly known as "Beecher's Bibles," for antislavery settlers in Kansas.

But Harriet never joined any abolitionist groups. Her passion was writing.

Loss of a Child

In Cincinnati, Harriet met and later married Calvin Stowe, a professor of languages and biblical studies at her father's seminary. Calvin was attracted by Harriet's lively intelligence, and he vigorously supported her writing career (which supplemented their income and later earned them more money than his own work did). When she began to publish her stories, he wrote to her, "My dear, you must be a literary woman." Harriet and Calvin eventually had seven children.

In 1849, while Calvin was away, a cholera epidemic broke out in Cincinnati. The disease causes severe diarrhea, and people die for lack of fluid in their bodies. At first the disease seemed to be confined to the poorer parts of town, but it soon spread to the Stowes' house and to their eighteen-month-old child, Charley.

After suffering for three agonizing days, Charley died. Harriet wrote: "Never was he anything to me but a comfort. He has been my pride and joy. . . . Many an anxious night have I held him to my bosom and felt the sorrow and loneliness pass out of me with the touch of his little warm hands."

Years later, outlining how she came to write *Uncle Tom's Cabin*, Stowe explained: "It was at *his* dying bed, & at *his* grave, that I learnt what a poor slave mother may feel when her child is torn away from her. In the depths of sorrow, which seemed to me immeasurable, it was my only prayer to God that . . . this crushing of my own heart might enable me to work out some great good to others."

Writing *Uncle Tom's Cabin*

It took a bad law to inspire Stowe to perform this "great good." In 1850, the U.S. Congress passed the Fugitive Slave Act. Slave owners had always been able to bring back runaways from the free states, but this new law made that task easier. The captive had no right to a trial, so anyone could turn in any black person, even a free black, to claim a reward. Federal marshals could even force a citizen of a free state to assist in capturing a runaway slave. And anyone who offered a runaway help, like food or shelter, could be punished with a fine or jail time.

Even antislavery moderates, who favored gradual abolition, were enraged. How could a law force them to go against their conscience and help recapture slaves? Stowe's sister-in-law Isabella filled her letters with horror stories of fugitives hiding in attics and cellars and of slave families torn apart as some members escaped to Europe or Canada. One runaway fled to Canada in the dead of winter and lost both feet to frostbite.

The Stowes themselves sheltered a runaway for a night in Brunswick, Maine, where they had recently moved. "Now our beds were all full, & before this law passed I might have tried to send him somewhere else—As it was all hands in the house united in making him up a bed," Harriet wrote to her sister Catharine.

Caught up in the furor over this new law, Stowe sent the *National Era* a tale of a farmer whom God punishes for refusing to help a family of runaway slaves. The publisher asked her for more. Isabella encouraged her, writing, "Now, Hattie, if I could use a pen as you can, I would write something that would make this whole nation feel what an accursed thing slavery is."

In later years, one of Stowe's children described the scene this way: Isabella's letter was read in the parlor, and Stowe "rose up from her chair, crushing the letter in her hand, and with an expression on her face that stamped itself on the mind of her child, said: 'I will write something. I will if I live.'"

She didn't write something immediately. But a few months later, in February 1851, Stowe was in church when she suddenly had a vision of the death of her main character, Uncle Tom. As soon as she returned home, she put pen to paper to record what she had seen. When she read the scene aloud, her children broke into tears, and one of the boys said, "Oh, Mamma! Slavery is the most cruel thing in the world."

A month later, she wrote to the editor of the *National Era*, Gamaliel Bailey, proposing a series of installments for a story about a slave. "Up to this year I have always felt that I had no particular call to meddle with this subject, and I dreaded to expose even my own mind to the full force of its exciting power," she revealed. "But I feel now that the time is come when even a woman or a child who can speak a word for freedom and humanity is bound to speak."

Impact of *Uncle Tom's Cabin*

President Lincoln may have been exaggerating when he said that *Uncle Tom's Cabin* "made this great war," but it certainly did affect public opinion. It addressed itself to people who most likely wouldn't have read the serious memoirs that former slaves like Frederick Douglass wrote about their lives in bondage. But even people who hadn't read *Uncle Tom's Cabin* were influenced by it. The butchers, firefighters and newspaper boys who often made up the notorious mobs that broke up abolition rallies went to the Tom plays, and some had their minds changed. The abolitionist paper *The Liberator* reported, "O, it was a sight worth seeing, those ragged, coatless men and boys in the pit (the very *material* of which mobs are made) cheering the . . . antislavery sentiments!"

A visitor from Britain, the economist Nassau William Senior, said the effect of the plays on the common people in the North was so powerful that it altered how they reacted to the Fugitive Slave Act. Where once "the lower classes in New York and Boston enjoyed the excitement of a negro hunt as much as [England's] rustics enjoy following a fox hunt," by the time federal troops attempted to return Anthony Burns to slavery in 1854, nearly fifty thousand people lined the streets of Boston shouting, "Kidnapper! Slave Catcher! Shame! Shame! Shame!" Senior went on to say, "The attempt will not be repeated. As far as the Northern States are concerned, 'Uncle Tom' has repealed the Fugitive Slave Law."

Stowe's radical message changed Americans' minds because in many ways the book spoke to their most cherished moral values. She addressed a Christian audience, who shared an understanding of the words *sin* and *redemption*. When Eva and Tom died, readers thought of the death of Jesus on the cross. Through the sacrifice of Eva and Tom, Stowe hoped to awaken readers to America's original sin—slavery—a sin Americans could redeem by freeing their slaves. Then America would become the ideal republic that Washington and Jefferson had envisioned. (That Washington and Jefferson themselves had been slave owners was not widely known at the time.)

The Americans Stowe was addressing viewed mothers as almost sacred, so she painted a searing picture of slave families broken apart. Eliza flees so she can keep Harry. Tom is torn away from his wife and child. One slave mother kills her newborn rather than let the baby grow up in slavery. And when another drowns herself after being wrenched from her child, Stowe speaks directly to her readers, in a voice dripping with sarcasm: "You can get used to such things, too, my friend; and it is the great object of recent efforts to make our whole northern community used to them, for the glory of the Union."

A century after the American Civil War, as the civil rights movement gained momentum in the United States, the reputation of *Uncle Tom's Cabin* suffered. Readers began to notice subtle racial prejudices in the book. Stowe's lighter-skinned slaves were smarter than those with darker skin, who were portrayed as simple and childlike. To arouse her readers' sympathy for her fugitives, Stowe gave Eliza a light complexion and her husband a "set of fine European features." Tom is righteous but unthreatening; even when the opportunity presents itself, he steadfastly refuses to murder Legree. His failure to resist enslavement repelled many civil rights supporters, who began to use the label

"Uncle Tom" to refer to a black person who passively accepts mistreatment. Yet in its own period, *Uncle Tom's Cabin* was the single most successful piece of antislavery propaganda precisely because it connected with 1850s readers, with all their racial fears and prejudices.

With her eye on these readers, Stowe ended her book with something resembling a sermon. She asked Southerners to look into their "secret souls" and acknowledge the "woes and evils, in this accursed system." She appealed to Northerners no longer to pass over slavery "in silence." She begged mothers to "pity the mother who has all your affections, and not one legal right to protect, guide, or educate, the child of her bosom!" She wrote: "There is one thing that every individual can do—they can see to it that *they feel right*. An atmosphere of sympathetic influence encircles every human being. . . . See, then, to your sympathies in this matter!"

European Tour

The astronomical sales of *Uncle Tom's Cabin* quickly made Stowe an international celebrity, and in 1853 she toured Great Britain. Crowds appeared wherever she went, even at train stations. In Glasgow, Scotland, she was greeted by two thousand people singing a hymn. Her brother Charles described the scene when Stowe entered London's Exeter Hall: "[T]hey first clapped and stomped, then shouted, then waved their hands and handkerchiefs, then stood up—and to look down from above, it looked like *waves* rising and the foam dashing up in spray." But since it was still improper for women to speak in public, her husband delivered her speech.

As popular as her book was overseas, she made no money at all on copies sold in Europe because of the way copyright laws worked in those days. To compensate her, many of her fans contributed to a "Penny Offering"—donating a penny each to the author. While some people told her to use the money however she chose, others asked her to spend it to help slaves. In Aberdeen, Scotland, she received money for the Underground Railroad, the secret network of abolitionists who helped runaway slaves escape to the North or to Canada, and in Edinburgh readers gave her a silver tray covered with cash. In the end, she carried home the equivalent of twenty thousand U.S. dollars—almost as much as Abraham Lincoln earned in a year. She also returned with the signatures of over half a million British women addressed to "the Women of the United States of America," urging them to raise their voices against slavery.

Further Activism

Stowe's war against slavery wasn't over. As Americans opened the West in the 1850s, people began to ask, "Will the new states be slave or free?" To stop a congressional bill that would have opened the Kansas and Nebraska territories to slavery, Stowe published "An Appeal to the Women of the Free States of America, on the Present Crisis in Our Country," urging women to circulate petitions, arrange lectures and do all they could, including praying, to halt the spread of slavery.

Violence soon broke out in Kansas between pro- and antislavery settlers. But the strife was not confined to the territories. In the Senate, Charles Sumner of Massachusetts, a friend of Stowe's and an antislavery campaigner, was savagely beaten by South Carolina's Preston Brooks, an ardent supporter of slavery.

It was during this stormy period that Stowe published her second antislavery novel, *Dred: A Tale of the Great Dismal Swamp*. Her new hero was no Uncle Tom; Dred was an angry rebel leader whose father, Denmark Vesey, an actual historical figure, had organized a slave rebellion in South Carolina in 1822 and was hanged for it. The book was not successful. Stowe wrote it too quickly, and Dred was not a convincing character. The novel was remarkable, though, because Stowe's sympathy for a rebel was something new for her.

Then in 1859, the radical abolitionist John Brown led two of his sons and nineteen other men on a violent raid, capturing the federal armory in Harpers Ferry, Virginia. He hoped to trigger a slave uprising, but federal troops shot their way into the armory, killing ten men and capturing seven, including Brown. Like many other Northerners who had once advised moderation, Stowe saw John Brown as a martyr—a "brave, good man who calmly gave up his life to a noble effort for human freedom." She had come a long way from the days of Uncle Tom.

Like the story of Stowe's meeting with President Lincoln, another story has come down to us. When asked how she came to write *Uncle Tom's Cabin*, Stowe answered, "God wrote it." Moved by two kinds of love—the love of a mother for her child, and the love of God for all humanity—she felt she was simply taking God's dictation.

"The nearer one gets to her face and to her mind, the more beautiful they are," American author Washington Irving wrote about Frances Anne Kemble.

CHAPTER 6

"So Grievous a Sin against Humanity"

Frances Anne Kemble

FOUR HUNDRED THIRTY-SIX PEOPLE, the youngest a fifteen-day-old baby, went on the auction block at a racetrack near Savannah, Georgia, on March 2, 1859. Pierce Butler sold the slaves in an act of desperation. He had squandered his money in bad investments and had to sell his most valuable possessions to raise the funds he needed to pay his debts and continue to live in luxury.

Before the sale, Butler's slaves had lived and worked on two plantations in Georgia—one that grew rice on Butler Island, and the other that grew cotton on St. Simons Island. These islands, just 15 miles (24 kilometers) apart, were the only home these slaves had ever known, and the only home their parents and grandparents had known. But now the slaves would have new owners and new homes, many of them far from Georgia.

Interested buyers examined the slaves as if they were animals. They walked around the shed in which they were housed, "pulling their mouths open to see their teeth, pinching their limbs to find how muscular they were, walking them up and down to detect any sign of lameness," wrote a reporter from New York.

Butler's sale became known as "the weeping time," which is what it was for the slaves. For Butler, it was a success. He raised more than three hundred thousand dollars, a fortune in the mid-nineteenth century, and perhaps to ease his conscience, he gave one dollar in coins to each slave as he said good-bye.

As the slaves left the racetrack, they could not have known that Pierce Butler's former wife, Frances Anne Kemble, would soon tell the world about them and their families. Her book *Journal of a Residence on a Georgian Plantation in 1838–1839*, published in 1863, describes the abject poverty, long workdays, daily degradations and harsh beatings she saw the slaves endure during her stay on the Georgia islands.

Read widely in America and Britain, Kemble's book was praised by people who hated slavery and criticized by those who supported it. In England, the Ladies' Emancipation Society printed hundreds of thousands of brochures with selections from the book in hopes of rallying the British people against the South during the American Civil War. In the United States, the book quickly went into a second printing and became a boon to the Northerners' cause. The New York reporter who'd written about Butler's slave auction hoped to capitalize on its popularity by reissuing his newspaper article as a pamphlet with the words "A Sequel to Mrs. Kemble's Journal" on the cover page.

Kemble was Butler's wife from June 7, 1834, until September 22, 1849, when they divorced. She had lived on the islands with him and their two daughters, Sarah and Frances, from late December 1838 until mid–April 1839. She would have known some of the slaves who were sold at the auction, as well as their parents and grandparents.

Family Life

Frances Anne Kemble, known to her family and admirers as Fanny, became an abolitionist through an unlikely route. She was born into a family of celebrated British actors on November 27, 1809. Her father's parents performed onstage, and at one time or another their six children all did as well, including Kemble's father, Charles, an acclaimed Shakespearean actor.

Fanny's mother, Maria Theresa Decamp Kemble (also known as Marie Thérèse De Camp Kemble), began her theatrical career when she was only six years old. She entertained by singing, dancing and performing for wealthy members of society. When she was twelve, her father died, and Maria Theresa became her family's main wage earner.

Fanny, however, did not seem destined for the stage. Her interests were reading, writing, lively conversation and vigorous activity. She loved walking (even in bad weather), riding horses, fishing and dancing. And she prized her independence.

Writing was a passion and also a family tradition. Kemble's parents had written plays, and other relatives had published poetry, essays and literary criticism. Fanny was confident that she too could succeed through her pen. But her plans were derailed by the family's financial problems.

In 1820 her father took over management of the struggling Covent Garden Theatre in London from his older brother, John. He proved to be no more successful in restoring the theater to health, and the financial situation turned particularly grim in the summer of 1829. While Charles was on tour in Ireland, performing and searching for an actress who would bring success to Covent Garden, creditors posted FOR SALE signs on the theater and began to call for the debts to be paid.

Maria Theresa, who had helped her own family when she was a girl, thought her daughter might be the Kembles' savior. She asked her to learn two Shakespearean roles, and when Charles returned home, Fanny performed Juliet in *Romeo and Juliet* for him. A few days later, he asked her to accompany him to the theater to see if her voice was powerful enough to reach the back rows. It was, and Fanny wrote years later that she was enthralled by the wonderful play as her "voice resounded through the great vault above and before me."

On Stage

After that, things happened quickly. In October 1829, a month shy of her twentieth birthday, Fanny Kemble made her debut as Juliet. Her mother took the stage after a twenty-year absence to play Juliet's mother, and her father performed the role of Romeo's friend Mercutio. Every seat was taken, with theater lovers and the curious eager to see the new leading lady. Rousing cheers greeted Fanny as she took the stage, but that was nothing compared to the joyous ovation that echoed as she took her bows. The reviews were sensational. "We do not remember to have ever seen a more triumphant debut," wrote *The Times*, a London newspaper.

Such accolades assured sell-out crowds and Fanny's fame. "From an insignificant school-girl, I had suddenly become an object of general public interest," she wrote a friend just three weeks after her debut. Yet in spite of her success, she never enjoyed acting. Her father began to talk about earning money by touring America; Fanny hated the very thought of going there but said she would accompany him.

In August 1831, Charles and Fanny, with Fanny's aunt Adelaide Decamp as an escort, boarded the ship the *Pacific* for their month-long journey to New York. En route and once in America, Fanny wrote letters to friends and family and kept a journal of observations. These tell about the ocean voyage, her theatrical life, her surroundings and her daily life—the markets, the trees, the flowers, the insects and the people. She found America very different from Britain and was shocked and dismayed at the treatment of blacks. "The prejudice against these unfortunate people is of course incomprehensible to us," she wrote.

The Kembles followed a demanding schedule, with performances in major cities up and down the East Coast—from New York to Philadelphia and back again, on to Baltimore and Washington, up to Albany, to Boston and to Toronto in Canada. They played to exuberant audiences everywhere. A critic from the *New-York Evening Post* commented that Fanny showed "an intensity and a truth never exhibited by an actress in America, certainly never by one so young."

Philadelphia was quiet after New York, but Fanny enjoyed the peace. Several young men visited her, and one of them, Pierce Butler, paid particular attention. Born into a wealthy Philadelphia family in 1806, Butler gave every appearance of being a wealthy Northern gentleman. With his accent and mannerisms, his connection with the South was not obvious, but the family's wealth came from his grandfather's plantations in Georgia. He and his brother were next in line to inherit the estates upon the death of an elderly aunt. Until then, he was free to do as he chose, and he chose to spend his days with Fanny.

He knew of her love of the outdoors and offered to find her the best riding horses possible. He accompanied her on her rides, read poetry with her, saw her stage performances, and on her return to town after a second round of shows in New York, became a regular companion. He joined the Kembles as they continued their tour down to Washington and then north toward Canada. Butler was kind and charming, but Charles and Adelaide were concerned. They feared what marriage would mean for Fanny's career, and they wondered if Butler was the right man for her. Stories had reached them that he was of questionable character and reckless with money. Fanny later said that she was so in love, she ignored her aunt's warnings.

Fanny and Butler married in 1834, and she stopped acting, with no regrets. Because she was depriving her father of income, she signed over to him the interest on money she had invested in an American savings account. Charles returned to England alone. Adelaide had died earlier that year from injuries she suffered during a coach accident on their trip to Canada. The new bride was beginning her married life with no Kembles nearby and no theaters to save, but with plans to publish.

Fanny had adapted the diary she kept during the previous two years—from the day she embarked for America through her journey to Niagara Falls—into a book she titled *Journal of a Residence in America*. Though she could have kept the income from it, she donated her earnings to an unmarried aunt who was surviving on the meager income of a governess. Now married to a wealthy man, Kemble thought she was financially secure.

Marriage Woes

But her marriage was not a happy one. Kemble and Butler soon discovered that they were profoundly different. Butler believed that a husband's word was law, and that his wife should do exactly what he said. His ideas were not unusual for a nineteenth-century man, but they were hateful to Kemble.

Her husband and his family criticized her flamboyant and unconventional clothes, and found fault with many of her friends. Butler no longer wanted to read with her or ride with her. He also wanted her to cancel the contract for her book, but the publisher would not allow it. She agreed to let Butler edit it but resented the changes he made. He removed references to slavery and jokes about America, and the more he deleted, the angrier she got.

Kemble, who detested slavery, had not known before her marriage that the Butler family owned slaves and had become wealthy from their hard work. In 1835 she wrote to a friend that even if it meant she had to go back to "toilsome work tomorrow," she would gladly do that rather than benefit from "so grievous a sin against humanity."

As the *Journal of a Residence in America* neared publication, she wrote "a long and vehement treatise against Negro slavery" to add to it. Warned, probably by Butler, that her words would incite proslavery mobs to tear down their house and burn their furniture, she omitted that section. But she did not keep silent about her views. She spoke out at social gatherings as well as in her personal letters, upsetting the Butlers, who were outraged that she was disobedient and publicly embarrassing.

The family insisted that she was wrong about slavery, that it was good for slaves to be under the control and discipline of whites, and that the Butlers were kind masters. In 1836, Pierce's aunt died, and he and his brother became joint owners of the plantations and the slaves on St. Simons and Butler islands. They intended to control the estates as their aunt had, as absentee owners. A manager would be in charge in Georgia, while they continued to live in Philadelphia, with one or the other of them visiting occasionally to check on things. That plan didn't suit Kemble. She wanted to join Butler for an extended stay so she could judge slavery for herself. She didn't get her way until two years later.

Journal of a Residence on a Georgian Plantation

The Butlers left Philadelphia in December 1838 with their two daughters, four-year-old Sarah and infant Frances (called Fan), and the children's nurse. During each day of their journey and their nearly sixteen-week stay, Kemble recorded her observations and reflections on life in a slave society. She wrote these accounts as if they were letters and addressed them to her friend Elizabeth Sedgwick, who lived in Massachusetts. Often Kemble wrote in a rush, jotting down incomplete thoughts. She did not deliver the letters to her friend until long after she had left Georgia.

Her first letter was from Philadelphia, before the journey even began. It is her response to accusations that she was going to the plantations prejudiced against what she would find there. "I *am* going prejudiced against slavery," she admitted, "for I am an Englishwoman, in whom the absence of such a prejudice would be disgraceful," but she went on to say that she was also prepared to find much kindness. She promised that she would accurately report what she saw.

The Georgia *Journal* includes what she saw and heard, what the slaves told her, what the white overseers told her, and what Butler told her. Kemble asked the slaves questions about their lives and gained an understanding vastly different from the perspective of the slave owners she met. She wrote about all of this.

The family stayed first on Butler Island, where Kemble quickly learned that the slaves were as curious about her as she was about them. When she tried to take a walk, they surrounded her, touching her clothes and complimenting her. When she returned to the house, they peered in the doorway, watching her and her children.

Kemble was accustomed to having servants assist her around the house, so it was nothing new to have a cook, a laundrywoman, a housemaid and two footmen. What was new was that they were filthy, and she was appalled. "Their faces, hands, and naked feet [were] literally encrusted with dirt," Kemble wrote about the footmen. White Southerners claimed that these slovenly habits were characteristic of the race and proof of their inferiority and need for enslavement, but Kemble said all the evidence showed that slavery was to blame. Self-respect contributes to cleanliness and personal attention, and there is no self-respect in being a slave, she said.

Most of the slaves on the Butler plantations worked from dawn to dusk in the rice or cotton fields. These field hands headed to their work at sunrise, carrying with them the grains they would cook for their meals. They labored until noon, then stopped and made a fire to cook their breakfast, often a very thick porridge. They then continued working at least six more hours, without a break, until they could prepare their second meal. The pattern varied little for slaves with different jobs. Outside the mill, where the rice plants were processed, workers sat wherever they could to eat. There were no chairs, so some sat on doorsteps and others on the ground. There were no plates, so they ate out of little wooden tubs or an iron pot. Lacking forks and knives, children used their hands and adults ate with broken iron spoons, pieces of wood or their fingers.

The sleeping accommodations were just as bad. The men who worked in the Butlers' house curled up on the floor near the kitchen fire at night; the women rested on a bedstead covered with tree moss to soften it. In the North, Kemble wrote, even the worst and poorest servants would not stick with a job if they had to work in the conditions routinely forced upon slaves.

But Kemble's greatest outrage was over the conditions in the infirmary. There, "on the floor, without bed, mattress, or pillow, buried in tattered and filthy blankets," lay slaves ill with fever, mothers about to give birth and people aching with rheumatism. These conditions prevailed, she wrote, in "the hospital of an estate where the owners are supposed to be humane, the overseer efficient and kind, and the Negroes remarkably well cared for and comfortable."

Wherever she went around the island, she asked the slaves about themselves. Seeing that she was interested and sympathetic, the women, in particular, felt comfortable speaking to her. But both men and women remarked that she spoke to them in a way no other white person had.

Sometimes her attention got slaves in trouble. On a visit to the infirmary, she urged mothers caring for ill babies to keep them clean. Harriet, one of the slaves, said that they were just so tired after working from dawn to evening that all they could do was sleep. Kemble reported this to the overseer, the white employee who supervised the slaves. He adamantly denied what Harriet had said. The next day, when Kemble returned to the infirmary, she found Harriet crying. The overseer had whipped her for complaining, she said. When Kemble told her husband about this, she declared that she would not be able to stay if people were punished for things they said to her. She could not hear their complaints without trying to make things better for them. Butler said she should not believe anything the slaves told her, and the overseer said Harriet had been whipped for shirking her duties. Kemble was not convinced but dropped the subject.

The family moved to St. Simons Island after seven weeks, and there life was no better for the slaves. On just one day, Kemble noted that nine women came to her with sad stories and pathetic requests, including the following:

Fanny has had six children, but only one is still alive. She asked Kemble to have her work in the field lightened.

Nanny has had three children; two of them are dead. She appealed to Kemble for a change in the rule that mothers be sent into the field three weeks after giving birth.

Sophy, Lewis's wife, asked for some old linen. Kemble wrote that she was suffering fearfully and that only five of her ten children have survived. The principal favor Sophy requested was a piece of meat, which Kemble gave her.

Charlotte, Renty's wife, had had two miscarriages, and was pregnant again. She was almost crippled with rheumatism, and Kemble's heart ached on seeing her poor swollen knees. She promised to make her a pair of flannel trousers.

Butler became increasingly convinced that Kemble was undermining the slaves' morale. The slaves were all liars, he said, and she should not listen to them or bother him with their complaints. She began to wonder if she was actually making things harder for them by giving them hope that life would improve. "[I]nstead of really befriending them," she wrote, "I am only preparing more suffering for them whenever I leave the place, and they can no more cry to me for help."

But she could not ignore their suffering and found ways to alleviate what she called their "really *beastly* existence." For example, the slaves had no church of their own and could attend services only once a month. The overseer severely flogged one slave who allowed his wife to be baptized. Religion was on Kemble's mind when she wrote, "There is not a single natural right that is not taken away from these unfortunate people." When her husband had to leave St. Simons Island for Butler Island, Kemble allowed slaves to come to the house for prayer readings on Sunday mornings. Typically, twenty or thirty attended.

Most troubling for Kemble was that the slaves accepted the Southerners' view that they were inferior to whites. As long as they thought that, she did not see how they could progress.

One time, she asked some of the male slaves to take her, her daughters and their nurse to Little St. Simons Island, a densely forested barrier island nearby. The route she suggested they follow took most of the day. The slaves had to cut a path through the woods, and they traveled by foot and cart along mosquito-infested sea swamps, marshes and burning wood. Only after she was muddied and exhausted from the trek did she realize that they could have traveled more quickly and easily if they had gone by boat when the tide was high. She was sure the slaves realized that, since they had lived in the area all their lives. She asked one of them why he hadn't suggested it, and he replied that she had said to go through the woods, so he would not tell her to go another way. That kind of sub-servience is typical of slavery, Kemble wrote. Slaves are so oppressed, tyrannized and degraded that they begin to see themselves the way their tormentors do. Their owners tell them they have little value as people, and so they believe their thoughts are not worth mentioning.

It was unusual for Kemble to find a slave admitting that he wanted to improve, but in her last week in Georgia, sixteen-year-old Aleck did just that. He asked her to teach him to read. She got him started, although teaching slaves was against state law. A person caught doing so could be fined for the first offense, fined even more for a second offense and imprisoned if caught a third time. She would gladly suffer prison for something she considered so right and impor-tant, she said.

When the Butlers returned to Philadelphia, Kemble began to revise her journal for publication. She re-read the notes, explaining as needed, smoothing the language and filling in gaps. When her husband was preparing to leave for Georgia the next year, she asked to join him so that she could expand the journal and clarify her observations, but he refused to let her go.

She circulated the journal privately to some abolitionists, and one of them, Lydia Maria Child, asked to publish parts of it in her periodical, the *National Anti-Slavery Standard*. Butler would not allow it, and Kemble obeyed him. She thought it would be a violation of his privacy if she revealed things about his plantations without his consent.

End of a Marriage

Tensions between the couple remained high. In the summer of 1844, Butler took the girls to Newport, Rhode Island, without Kemble. On his return, he allowed Kemble only minimal time with Sarah and Fan and denied her any say in their upbringing. By February 1845, he forbade her even to see the children.

With her children lost to her, she returned to England, and in 1849 Kemble and Butler were divorced. This was rare in those years, and courts gave pref-erential treatment to men. The couple's agreement gave Kemble an annual income, two months with their daughters each year and unlimited contact with them by letter. She dropped the "Butler" from her name, calling herself Mrs. Frances Anne Kemble.

Kemble did not discuss the divorce publicly and included nothing about it in her journals. Others were more open with their views. A friend of Butler's, who blamed Kemble for the breakup, wrote, "Everybody knew that the lady was an uncompromising abolitionist . . . on the *one subject* she was a hopeless monomaniac"—meaning she was fanatical.

Once back in England, an ocean away from her husband and children, she could have published the journal, but she feared that Butler would deny her contact with her daughters. To earn money, she resumed acting for a short time and then toured England giving Shakespearean readings. She looked forward to Sarah's and Fan's twenty-first birthdays, in 1859 and 1861, when they would be free to see their mother as often as they liked.

Hard times came to Butler before that. He began losing money in 1856, and by 1859 he had to sell his slaves.

Publication of the Georgia *Journal*

Finally, in 1863, Kemble decided the time was right for publication of her *Journal of a Residence on a Georgian Plantation*. Two years earlier, the Southern states had seceded from the Union, and North and South were embroiled in the Civil War. "The ignorant and mischievous nonsense I was continually compelled to hear upon the subject of slavery in the seceding States determined me to publish my own observation of it," Kemble later wrote. She did not expect the book to change any minds, but she wanted to testify to the horrors of the system.

At the recommendation of friends, she closed the book with a letter she had written for *The Times* in 1852 but never mailed. In the book, she wrote that she was convinced the London newspaper would not have published it. But she may also have delayed publication because she feared that if the letter had been printed, Butler might have blocked her access to the children. Her letter was a response to articles about Harriet Beecher Stowe's *Uncle Tom's Cabin*, which Kemble called "the most popular and most hated book of the day." *The Times*, she wrote, was wrong to call the novel "an exaggerated picture of the evils of slavery." As an eyewitness to slavery, she could attest to the fact that Stowe's book depicted it faithfully.

Just as America was split over slavery, so were Kemble's daughters, with Sarah opposed and Fan supporting it. They did not agree about the Georgia *Journal* either. Fan considered it a betrayal of her father and disrespectful to their family, while Sarah, who was part of a writing circle that aided abolitionist causes, thought it persuasive.

Reviewers of the book were divided along similar lines. Those who sympathized with the Northern cause regarded the book as an honest and eloquent account of the pain and despair of slavery. Allies of the South criticized the book for its depiction of the Southern states and its factual errors.

Questions about accuracy would haunt the book for decades to come. In 1959, a New York publishing company faced fierce opposition from a historian of St. Simons Island when it announced that it would reissue the book. The historian's critique of the *Journal* appeared in *The Georgia Historical Quarterly*, and others joined the attack, pointing to Kemble's factual errors to undermine the book's credibility. But that didn't stop the publisher, who released the new edition in 1961.

There are some errors in the book, but they are minor. Writing quickly and with no chance to return to the plantations and revisit people, Kemble got some names wrong. A slave she called Scylla was actually named Sinder, for example, and a duel that took place before her stay she described as occurring while she was in Georgia. Still, the substance of the book is correct. A Philadelphia friend of the Butlers, a supporter of slavery, wrote in his diary that Butler's sister-in-law, Gabriella, had told him the book was accurate. Gabriella, he wrote, "says Mrs. Kemble's description of the treatment of the Negroes & their condition on the Butler estate is true, & she ought to know as she owns half the property, or did before the war, & has frequently resided on the estate." Decades later, when historians looked at the Butler family historical papers, they found them consistent with the *Journal*.

The book remained a sore point with Fan for years. In 1882, when her mother published *Records of a Later Life*, a memoir of her marriage and subsequent years, Fan hoped to undermine it by releasing *Ten Years on a Georgia*

Plantation Since the War. That book describes her attempts to restore the family's estates to grandeur. Fan's aim was to redeem her father's reputation, although her book addresses a time forty years after her mother left Georgia. Despite Fan and Fanny's disagreement, mother and daughter remained on good terms.

Kemble's *Journal*, like Kemble herself, was passionate and sincere. It helped build the case against slavery by documenting its horrific effects in personal terms. Kemble's strength was that she saw the slaves as individuals and treated them that way. Aleck, whom she instructed in reading, eventually learned to read and write. Long after Kemble's death in 1893, he was still corresponding with her daughter Sarah, who had returned to Philadelphia.

Despite the dangers in the Congo region, Alice Seeley Harris developed trusting relationships with local people and even ventured into the bush.

Alice Harris's photograph of Nsala grieving over his daughter's hand and foot ignited the outrage that ended King Leopold's exploitation of the people of the Congo.

CHAPTER 7

"They Are Women As You and I Are"

Alice Seeley Harris

On a Sunday morning in May 1904, Alice Seeley Harris, a young Englishwoman, was at home in an African mission with a visitor, the missionary Edgar Stannard. Harris had moved to the Congo with her husband, John, six years earlier, intending to educate the native people and convert them to Christianity.

That day, Harris's husband was away, and she and Stannard were about to begin their morning prayers when two young African boys ran in, out of breath, with the news that some local people had been murdered by sentries (Congolese soldiers appointed by white officials to control the native community).

The boys told Harris and Stannard that witnesses were on their way to report the murders to the "rubber white men," the Belgians who ran the rubber trading company in the area. Knowing that the Harrises often sided with the locals against abuses by the sentries, the boys had come to their house with the news.

Later the witnesses arrived and told Harris and Stannard their story. Stannard repeated it a few days later in a letter to the director of the Congo Balolo Mission:

Thereupon one of them opened a parcel of leaves, and showed us the hand and foot of a small child, who could not have been more than five years old. They were fresh and clean cut. It was an awful sight, and even now, as I write, I can feel the shudder and feeling of horror that came over me as we looked at them, and saw the agonised look of the poor fellow, who seemed dazed with grief, and said they were the hand and foot of his little girl. I can never forget the sight of that horror-stricken father.

The sentries who had committed this terrible crime had also killed the child's mother and eaten them both. (Cannibalism was a common practice in the Congo region at the time, shocking as this is for us to understand today.)

Though not a professional photographer, Alice Seeley Harris had a professional's instinct. She immediately wanted to document the atrocity. Since arriving in Africa, she had developed considerable skill at taking pictures, and now, faced with a crime of this enormity, she collected her photographic equipment. She asked the father, Nsala, to sit on the veranda of their bungalow and look directly at the hand and foot of his murdered daughter, Boali. Then she took the picture.

When her husband saw her photograph, he praised "the promptness & courage she showed in getting such a picture under such circumstances, as every minute might have brought the traders to the spot." The Belgian rubber traders didn't want atrocities like these exposed in Europe and America, which is precisely what Alice Harris's photographs did. They created such an uproar that they helped turn the tide of public opinion against the conduct of the Belgian rubber traders in Africa.

Becoming Missionaries

Alice Seeley Harris went to Africa with religion in mind, not political affairs. Her interest in the continent began when, as a young girl, she heard her father talk about the missionary David Livingstone and the explorer Henry Morton Stanley. Later, when she worked in the British civil service, she came under the influence of F.B. Meyer, the London-based preacher for the Regions Beyond Missionary Union, and decided to join the Congo Balolo Mission. The preacher "was very keen on missionary work and did everything to encourage young people to offer themselves," she told a BBC interviewer in 1970, when she was one hundred years old. "And as soon as I did, my parents objected. I had to wait seven years." It took a marriage proposal from another young missionary, John Hobbis Harris, to convince her father to let her go. They married on May 6, 1898, and left four days later for the Congo.

The Congo Free State

The Congo at this time was under the control of a European king, Leopold II of Belgium. He had named it the *État Indépendant du Congo* in French; in English, it was called the Congo Free State. But there was nothing free or independent about it. King Leopold's colony was founded on one principle: raw greed. Belgian administrators enslaved native Congolese, starving them, uprooting them from their villages and working them to death. This exploitation lined the pockets of Belgian ivory and rubber traders—and of Leopold II himself. The stories Alice's father had told her about Livingstone and Stanley did not prepare her for what she and John would encounter in Africa.

David Livingstone's book *Missionary Travels and Researches in South Africa*, published in 1857, had drawn attention to the Arab-led slave trade and traditional African slavery. At the same time, European governments became interested in exploring Africa and exploiting its natural wealth in ivory, minerals, rubber, palm oil and land. Missionaries traveled to Africa to Christianize the natives, wipe out the slave trade and end cannibalism. Merchants went to get rich.

At a conference held in Berlin in 1884–85, the European powers divided Africa into colonies. The Congo became King Leopold's private outpost, administered by Belgians. Promising to end the slave trade, Leopold sold the rights to set up rubber-trading stations along the Congo River to Belgians and other Europeans. The agents running those concessions would "tax" the natives by forcing them into the forests to extract sap from rubber trees, then split the profits on the sale of the rubber with King Leopold. His Congo colony made Leopold immensely rich, though he never set foot on African soil.

There was no other word for what the rubber workers became but slaves. They were forced into the bush with quotas of rubber to collect; if they did not meet these quotas, they were brutally beaten with a *chicotte*, a heavy rhinoceros whip that slashed their skin. To make the men show up for work, the overseers held their wives, children and elders as hostages, starving and thirsty, in huts; women were raped, children slaughtered, and sometimes all the hostages were burnt alive if a quota wasn't met. Sentries were encouraged to be as brutal as the Europeans. Villagers fled deeper and deeper into the bush, but they were usually tracked down and murdered by the sentries. To prove that they had not "wasted" bullets, the sentries cut off the right hands of their victims and showed them to the authorities.

By the 1890s, the truth about these crimes was leaking out to Europe and the United States. Missionaries were aware of many of these abuses, but though some confided their uneasiness to each other, for years they failed to go public for fear of losing the right to continue their work in the region.

At the Mission Station

By September 1900, the Harrises had settled at a missionary station in Baringa, 1,200 miles (1,900 kilometers) inland from the west coast of Africa. Alice set up a school. "I loved teaching them at school, and they enjoyed it themselves so much," she recalled in her BBC interview. "To see the [light] dawn in their faces, it was wonderful!"

Life in Baringa presented many dangers, however, and sometimes John Harris was away, leaving Alice to face them on her own. One morning, she awoke distressed. The other missionary at the station could tell something was wrong. "I said, 'Oh, I had a terrible night. I've been dreaming all night about a *mambatau* [a poisonous snake, also called a mamba].'" She slept in a protected tent "made of linen or calico and the sides . . . made of mosquito net. That was all," she told her interviewer. She went on:

> And the only light we had was a candle, so if I got a candle on the stool close by my bed, I had to lift up the mosquito net like this and slide my hand underneath to find the matches, but I always had to be careful about that. I might have touched anything without knowing it. I was just going to do it again as usual . . . and . . . something or someone said to me, "Don't!" and I didn't.

Her husband's assistant came to the tent to see if she needed help. Suddenly, he called out, "My word! There's a mamba!"

"It came out from under the bed," Harris remembered. "This black mamba came and I'd been sitting there. . . . I had no doubt that that snake was there every time I saw it in my dream." The assistant sent his servant for a gun, then "fired so accurately he shot the head clean off."

Relationships between missionaries and Africans could also present challenges. One time Alice and John were visiting a local chief when the gun John was teaching him to use recoiled, frightening their host. The Harrises concluded that the incident made the chief suspicious of them. Alice said:

> Our natives had heard [some of our hosts] talking during the night; perhaps they were going to have a feast off us. So although we needed the rest so badly and intended resting that Sunday, we walked from early morning till late at night so we were well out of their reach. I've often been surprised myself since, and wondered how calmly we did the things that we did.

Alice was touched by the hard lives she witnessed in Africa. She once took in an abandoned child she found wandering, starved and covered in sores. Then the couple had their own first child in Africa, and they returned to England in May 1901 for a year's leave. Another child was born in England, but in May 1902 the Harrises decided to return to Africa, even though it meant leaving their children at the mission children's home in London.

"Rubber Is Death"

Baringa was the largest rubber-collecting district in the Congo Free State, and locals often went to the Harrises with reports of mistreatment, knowing the missionaries would try to help. When Nsala brought his daughter's hand and foot to the mission station, Alice followed up with a formal letter of complaint to Raoul Van Calcken, the director of the rubber station. "We have seen the hand and foot of the child, Boali, who with her mother was eaten by the sentries or their dependants," she wrote. "We have heard that almost all the people who were killed and eaten, and also those who remain imprisoned, are women. . . . [I]t is absolutely illegal to imprison women for the purpose of bargaining over rubber." She asked him to report these crimes to the appropriate authorities.

The Anglo-Belgian India Rubber Company (ABIR) struck back. The director ordered local villages not to sell supplies to the Harrises, and by June 1904, they were surviving on canned food and goat milk. Two months later, John Harris wrote home that Van Calcken had ordered guns to be fired in the vicinity of the mission station, presumably to intimidate the Harrises into silence. If that was Van Calcken's intention, it did not work. Soon after, Alice sent her first grisly photos home.

Responding to public criticism, King Leopold established a commission of inquiry into allegations of atrocities in the rubber trade. The king handpicked the investigators, expecting them to back his regime. But Leopold's plan backfired when John brought witnesses to testify before the commission, and the king's own appointees found it impossible to whitewash the Congo crimes. They issued a scathing report in 1905.

At one point the Harrises heard rumors of a massacre in Bongwonga, a village in the region where they worked, and decided to travel there with their camera to locate survivors and take testimony. The result was a pamphlet called *Botofé Bo Le Iwa (Rubber Is Death)*. By choosing a Congolese proverb as their title, John and Alice were signaling that they were speaking for the Bongwonga people. Though the pamphlet is signed by John Harris, he made it known that Alice had collaborated with him in writing it. It also includes one of her photos, showing a line of Bongwonga rubber workers, each holding a basket to fill with his quota of rubber.

The Harrises published the pamphlet in London in 1906, after returning to England to publicize Congo atrocities. *Rubber Is Death* starts off calmly, describing the Congo's geography and the drastic decline in population under Belgian rule. Then, under the heading "Terror Is the Pivot Upon Which the Whole Congo Regime Turns," the Harrises document the horrors.

The stories told are so chilling that they're painful to read, yet the Harrises omit the most horrific events, stating: "It is impossible to print details of all tortures perpetrated on Congo natives. No journal would publish them for they reek with unheard-of filthiness and inhumanity; the mind must imagine them."

The Harrises let the facts speak for themselves, even when addressing a subject as chilling as cannibalism: "Banjanga—a man—killed and eaten. Litama and her son, Kaketa, killed and eaten." Another story describes how a worker named Bafuka was punished when his rubber haul was one basket short of the quota. Write the Harrises:

> Bafuka was eating caterpillars in his hut. Lonkumjo asks, "Why is the rubber short? You have been getting caterpillars instead of searching for rubber." He thereupon calls to his "boys," and tells them to tie the poor fellow to a tree. "Lonkumjo, do not shoot him, leave him to us," said the "boys." Spears were then run through his stomach, and his head cut off and placed on a stake near his house.

Having laid out their evidence objectively, the Harrises close with a passionate appeal: "Reader, as you picture this evil, remember that it is going on TODAY—that those defenseless men are being exterminated daily—that the still more defenseless women are suffering untold misery—untold because men cannot, dare not in this, the twentieth century, completely draw aside the veil."

The Congo Reform Association

In England, the Harrises joined the newly formed Congo Reform Association (CRA). They were in great demand as speakers, giving more than three hundred lectures in their first year. Alice's pictures were the highlight of the presentations. Sixty of them were converted to lantern slides, small squares of glass that were projected onto a screen or wall. Twelve of these were photographs of brutalities—people with amputated limbs, others in shackles—giving vivid and unmistakable proof of the horrors in the Congo, and leaving an indelible impression on the audience.

The Harrises couldn't keep up with the requests for them to speak, so they created a lantern-slide package that ministers could use in their Sunday sermons. At a Harris lecture in Wales, one woman was so moved that she donated her jewels to Alice to raise money for the CRA. The couple also toured the United States, speaking in forty-nine cities; in Chicago, one African-American woman, born a slave, offered her life savings to the Harrises, who would take only a dollar.

The lectures usually lasted an hour, with Alice's photographs of atrocities shown at the halfway mark. Near the end, slides of John standing beside an African chief and of natives making bricks and producing palm oil made the point that with European help, Africans were capable of doing productive work in a modern economy. To inspire listeners to support the CRA's struggle against slavery, the program closed on a religious note with a "Congo hymn" like this one:

> *Britons, awake!*
> *Let righteous ire*
> *kindle within your soul a fire,*
> *let indignation's sacred flame*
> *burn for the Congo's wrongs and shame.*

Alice's photographs continued to appear in pamphlets too. *The Camera and the Congo Crime*, also written by the Harrises, tells the same story as *Rubber Is Death*, but with fewer words and more of Alice's pictures. Its stark and powerful photographs—more than half of them taken by Alice—puncture King Leopold's lies. For example, his words "Each step forward made by our people must mark an improvement in the condition of the natives" appear above two photographs of natives mutilated by sentries for not meeting their rubber quota.

Flipping through the pages of *The Camera and the Congo Crime*, a reader would see image after image of the Congo's devastation. A typical two-page spread contrasts the village of Lungunda before the arrival of the Belgians with an image of huts and trees burned to the ground and fields deserted. The caption reads, "The same Village arbitrarily destroyed in order to Plant Rubber."

King Leopold was a formidable enemy, however. He accused his critics of faking photos, and he issued documents that challenged their accusations. But Alice persisted in presenting the reality of the Congo to the British public.

Alice's Writings

Alice Harris was as eloquent in words as she was in pictures. She put her writing skills to work in yet another pamphlet, *Enslaved Womanhood of the Congo:*

An Appeal to British Women, which was issued by the CRA around 1908. Its only picture is a striking close-up photograph of three somber Congolese women chained by their necks.

Harris opens her pamphlet by asking her readers, "Why should the women of England, as women, take up the Congo women's cause?" Because, she answers, the suffering from King Leopold's regime falls upon women and children. Her aim, she says, is to "set womanhood thinking and then resolutely acting towards ending a wrong and thereby saving a race."

To make the case against King Leopold, Harris marshals eyewitness accounts and statistics, systematically laying out evidence of a range of abuses. Women are held as hostages, she asserts, quoting a 1904 British consul's report on Congo abuses. She writes:

> I found 2 sentries of the La Lulanga Co. guarding 15 women. . . . I asked if it was women's work to collect India-Rubber, [and one sentry] said—"No, that of course it was men's work." "Then why do you catch women?" I asked. "Don't you see[?]" was the answer. "If I catch their wives the husbands are anxious to have them home again and so the rubber is brought in quickly and right up to the mark." At nightfall the fifteen women in the shed were tied together either neck to neck or ankle to ankle.

Harris claims in the pamphlet that Belgians routinely engage in a slave trade in women, offering as proof a 1907 account of the price paid for the sale of seventy-five Congolese women by Congo State officials. Women, she adds, are also forced to raise food for the Congo's administrators. "The women must clear forest land, plant acres of manioca tuber, constantly weed the garden, then after a year dig up the tubers, soak them for many days, pound them with pestle and mortar, then boil and finally prepare for consumption," she writes. She even quotes missionaries' reports that the population of the region is plummeting because the women are so overworked that they "have practically ceased to bear children."

Like Harriet Beecher Stowe in *Uncle Tom's Cabin*, Harris reminds the women reading her appeal that there is no difference between African and English mothers: "They are women as you and I are; animated by the same instincts as their more civilized sisters. The babe needs the love and protection of the mother, without which it will languish and die; yet the infant is cruelly torn from the mother's breast and left to perish in the road." She tells her readers that they have the power to speak for the women in Africa.

She ends her pamphlet with a plea to her readers to do three things:

1. Join the Congo Reform Association.
2. Organize Public and Private Meetings.
3. Obtain and Circulate Literature.

By 1908, all the negative publicity was taking its toll, and King Leopold finally agreed to sell the Congo Free State to the government of Belgium. Three years later, the Harrises returned to the Congo on behalf of their own government. Britain wanted to be sure that conditions there had improved before it agreed to Belgium's right to govern the colony. The Harrises eventually reported that they had witnessed no atrocities and had seen "immense improvement."

When she was well into her sixties, Alice continued to speak out against injustice—against the enslavement of women in Portugal's African colonies and the lynchings of black men in South Africa and the United States. But it was as a young missionary with a camera that she had her greatest impact. Her powerful images raised an outcry that changed the course of history.

In 1933, King George V honored Kathleen Simon with the title Dame Commander of the British Empire (DBE) for her antislavery work.

Mui-tsai girls like this one, in a photograph taken around 1930, often had only rags for clothes. Kathleen Simon campaigned against their enslavement for years.

CHAPTER 8

"To Wipe the Dark Stain of Slavery from the Face of the World"

Kathleen Simon

LADY KATHLEEN SIMON AND HER HUSBAND, Sir John, knelt in a front pew of St. Botolph's Church in London at midnight on Wednesday, August 1, 1934. It was an unusual hour for an unusual assembly. Scores of people—black and white, the highborn and the low, clergymen and working people, singers, journalists and abolitionists—sat side by side to commemorate the hundredth anniversary of the Slavery Abolition Act, the law that called for the end of slavery in most British colonies.

Few present would ever forget the evening, one newspaper reported. Floodlights illuminated the outside of the church and the surrounding gardens. Inside, every seat was taken, and flags of Britain and its colonies hung throughout the brightly lit building. A racially diverse crowd was so rare in a London divided by race and class that news reports highlighted it. One journalist wrote, "The whole function was poignantly mixed. I sat between an inspector of the NSPCC [National Society for the Prevention of Cruelty to Children] and a negress in European clothes and stud earrings." Lady Simon had made a point of appealing for people of all colors and faiths to attend, writing in a leaflet, "Let us all, white and dark people together," unite at the church. And they did. The service began with the singing of "God Save the King" and followed with prayers, speeches, hymns and songs.

The August 1 gathering was one of the crowning events in a year's worth of activities to celebrate Britain's abolition of slavery. No one was more active in the events than Lady Simon. Everywhere she traveled—throughout England and Wales, and even to Brazil with her husband, who was then foreign secretary—she discussed slavery, its present as well as its past. The abolition movement began in Britain, she said, but the earlier abolitionists did not finish the job.

Just days after the church service, Lady Simon reminded the British people that there was still work to do. "Free men and women should never be content unless they have helped . . . to wipe the dark stain of slavery from the face of the world," she told *The Times*, a London newspaper. Slavery was gone from the British West Indies but not from the world. She delivered that message to people anywhere and everywhere, winning friends, supporters and critics.

Slavery, the Book

As the wife of Sir John Simon, a prominent figure in the British government, Kathleen Simon was well known. In 1929 she gained fame in her own right with publication of her book *Slavery*. It gave vivid, often horrifying, accounts of enslaved people, and sent shockwaves through Britain as the public learned that slavery still existed in places under British control, such as Hong Kong.

Book reviewers heaped praise on Simon. "This is an eloquent book and a brave book on a problem too many accept as solved," one wrote. Another called it "a cry from a woman's heart," and yet another said, "Simon has sounded a new rallying call. . . . [W]e are summoned to a new crusade. Dare we disobey?" That was exactly what Simon wanted to do: enlist readers in a crusade like the one British abolitionists had led more than a century earlier to end slavery in the British West Indies.

The book appeared three years after members of the League of Nations—an organization similar to today's United Nations—signed a treaty called the Slavery Convention, which was designed to end the slave trade and eradicate slavery as soon as possible. But despite this agreement, slavery was still practiced in some parts of the world, often blatantly.

Most British people didn't know this. If they thought about slavery at all, they thought of it as something from the past. Britain had abolished slavery in its West Indian colonies one hundred years earlier, and most people assumed it came to a crashing halt in other countries after the American Civil War, in 1865. When Simon's book appeared, readers learned that as many as six million people were enslaved throughout the world.

Chapter by chapter, Simon described people in bondage in different nations in Africa, Asia and South America. She used facts, figures and heartrending anecdotes to persuade her readers to care about suffering and oppression, wherever they occurred. She quoted people she knew her readers would trust: British government and military officials, foreign dignitaries and journalists from respected newspapers. She urged Britons to rise up against slavery, as they had one hundred years before. "I now ask every reader to consider carefully and impartially the facts set out in these pages," she wrote, "and then to ask the simple question: 'What can I do to help to set these millions of slaves free from their soul-destroying, body-destroying bondage?'" She made a compelling case for action in nearly a dozen countries, including China and Abyssinia (now called Ethiopia).

Child Slavery in China

Many Chinese people defended slavery, Lady Simon wrote, claiming it was a Chinese custom to protect poor children—a form of charity that outsiders did not understand. The slavery lasted until the children were only fifteen or twenty years old, the Chinese said, and few children were abused. Simon rejected each of these claims, contending that two million children were slaves in China. An innocent tradition? No abuse? No harm? Not true, she argued.

She noted that in a single blacksmith shop in Shanghai, British and Chinese detectives found more than thirty boys, hungry, overworked, in poor health and scarred from burns by hot iron rods. The children "were given only two meals of rice a day," said a news article she quoted, "and any lad who refused to work was handcuffed and suspended to a wall." One of the boys had been enslaved for nearly six years.

Impoverished parents often sold their children in hopes that the buyers would take better care of them. Demand was high for girls, and many as young as four or five became *mui-tsai* (a Chinese word for a slave girl that translates as "little younger sister"). Though some of these girls were treated as family members, most lived like slaves. If you hated slavery, Simon said, you had to hate the *mui-tsai* system. Quoting the Hong Kong–based Anti–Mui Tsai Society, she wrote:

> A slave is bought with money:
> A Mui Tsai is bought with money.

> A slave is not paid for labour:
> A Mui Tsai is not paid for labour.
> A slave can be re-sold:
> A Mui Tsai can be re-sold.

The well-being of these children had "special gravity and importance," Simon wrote, because *mui-tsai* slavery occurred on British soil. Hong Kong, a small island off the southeast coast of China, was a British colony, subject to British laws. Slavery had been illegal there since the island became a colony in 1841, but the law had no effect. Slavery continued. Simon implored the public to insist that the British government free the *mui-tsai*.

Slavery in Ethiopia

People in Ethiopia also excused slavery. Ethiopia was a Christian nation in Africa and a member of the League of Nations. When the League admitted it in 1923, it set one condition—that Ethiopia abolish slavery. But that didn't happen. Slavery there took many forms, Simon said, from "the little household slaves of the Christian priests to the wretched mutilated boys and girls who are carried across the sea and sold in the slave-markets of Arabia . . . to the suffering gang, yoked and chained together, and driven by the crack of the whip through the country or to the coast ports for sale as human merchandise."

Simon painted an equally ugly picture of slave raids. In the dark of night, armed men working for powerful Ethiopian families swooped into villages in Sudan, Italian Eritrea and French Somaliland, and "the entire saleable population, men, women and children, [was] carried off in chains," she quotes a British naval commander as saying. "For days they [were] marched towards the coast," he said, through the streets, for all to see. They were then forced onto sailing vessels and carried to southern Arabia—and slavery.

Some Ethiopian leaders got rich from slavery and had no interest in ending it. One of Ethiopia's rulers, Ras Tafari (later known as Emperor Haile Selassie), said he supported abolition but could not enforce it without the help of other Ethiopian leaders. Simon suggested a way. The League of Nations could send advisers to Ethiopia, she said, to make sure slavery and corruption came to an end. If they did, the League would invest in honest businesses run by the rulers, so that they would not have to attack their neighbors and capture their people. Financial independence is the first step toward freedom, she wrote. The enthusiastic support of the British people could make the plan work.

Many of Simon's readers were indeed enthusiastic. The leader of a group called the Derby Unemployed Men's Brotherhood wrote, "May I thank you for giving us such an important and startling document as *Slavery*? I wish it could be placed in the hands of every deep-thinking citizen."

Simon's Early Hatred of Slavery

Simon acquired a passion for freedom and a loathing for cruelty when she was a young girl in southeastern Ireland. Kathleen's parents taught her to love liberty and hate servitude. She became a nurse and worked in some of the most destitute areas of London, where she saw women struggle under the hardships of poverty.

Her interest in slavery started later, when she lived in the United States. She and her first husband, the physician Thomas Manning, moved to Tennessee in 1885, just twenty years after the end of the Civil War and the abolition of slavery in America. Tennessee had been a slave state and had fought on the losing side of the war. Long after slavery ended, the lingering effects of human ownership were evident in white people's degrading, ruthless, neglectful and violent behavior toward the recently freed slaves and their descendants. The heartless treatment of one young girl, Amanda, haunted Simon all her life.

Simon met Amanda in Knoxville, Tennessee, but the circumstances of the meeting are not explained in her book or other writings. In one account she says they met in a college hall, but she does not name the college or explain why they were there. She noticed Amanda standing apart from everyone else and offered her hand, saying, "My name is Kathleen, what is yours?" When Simon asked the others why they had excluded Amanda, they told her the girl had "black blood," meaning black ancestors. Amanda's light skin made her look white, but to Simon her race was irrelevant.

Many years after the event, Simon recounted the story to the black American writer and civil rights leader W.E.B. Du Bois. "I was quite bewildered and refused not to talk to her," she told him. The way young Amanda was shunned, coupled with the brutality of the prejudice she saw in America, inspired Simon to battle cruelty, injustice and oppression for the rest of her life, and in 1929, to dedicate the book *Slavery* to Amanda.

When Simon returned to England after her first husband's death, she rejoined the workforce. At some point, she became governess to the children of John Simon, a member of Parliament whose wife had died in 1902. During the First World War, when she was no longer working for him, Kathleen approached Lord Simon for help. Her son, Brian Manning, was a soldier with the British army and had become a prisoner of war in Germany. Their meeting led to a romance and their eventual marriage, in December 1917. She became Lady Simon and gained three stepchildren, and John acquired one, Brian.

In the Public Eye

Kathleen Simon joined John on the campaign trail as he urged voters to re-elect him to Parliament in 1918. Though a newcomer to election campaigns, she was tireless and passionate, shaking voters' hands, answering their questions and asking for their votes. But John came up short.

Still, he did not give up, nor did his wife. In 1922, he won a different seat in Parliament, remaining in office until 1940. Throughout John's career, Kathleen campaigned for him, often giving short speeches to women voters, "for she has personality," one of the newspapers reported.

Kathleen was persuasive with her husband as well. As an Irishwoman, she opposed the British government's hard line against her people's pleas for independence. She once told an audience how she cajoled her husband after he had gone to bed with a bad cold. She paced the room, crying to him. "'How can you lie there,' I said, 'while these dreadful things are being done in my country?' Then he got up and started on his campaign and never stopped." In fact, he called the British actions against Ireland "politically disastrous and morally wrong," an unusually outspoken comment for an English member of Parliament. And he later wrote about Kathleen, "No Member of Parliament ever owed more to a comrade than I did to her."

Her causes became his causes, including the one closest to her heart: fighting slavery. John wrote the preface to her book and sent copies to every ambassador and government minister in London. That helped Kathleen achieve one of her goals—greater involvement by the League of Nations. In 1931, the organization established the Committee of Experts on Slavery to investigate what progress had been made in eradicating slavery since the 1926 agreement was signed.

Speaking about *Slavery*

Kathleen Simon was a tireless activist for the Anti-Slavery Society even before her book was published, but afterward she became known as an authority on slavery. She crisscrossed England, speaking in large towns and small, north and south, even traveling into Scotland and Wales to attend meetings and give talks. She called for a "war on slavery" wherever it occurred. "Human dignity, human sympathy and human freedom [know] no geographical boundaries," she said.

On travels with her husband, Lady Simon spoke to government leaders in Brazil, India, Egypt, Italy, France and Switzerland. Everywhere she went, she gained members and raised money for the Anti-Slavery Society. Her goal in her speeches was the same as her goal in the book: to rally a "great international crusade" to support the League of Nations in abolishing slavery.

In 1930, she accompanied John to North America. In Toronto, she compared Ethiopian slavery with slavery in America. In Chicago, she lectured on slavery in Ethiopia, Arabia and China, and even criticized the United States. She drew parallels between the horrors of slavery in other countries and American lynchings (vigilante acts in which mobs of whites captured, tortured and killed blacks). Though slavery had been abolished in the United States, she said, "another shocking evil had grown up. . . . I cannot condemn America enough for tolerating such barbarity."

In New York she met with W.E.B. Du Bois, the African-American civil rights leader she had written to about young Amanda. Months earlier, he had faulted *Slavery* in a magazine article for relying too much on the reports of

British officials. It attacks "all the slave-holders in the world except the British," he wrote.

Harsh as his comments were, Simon did not seem to mind. "My only complaint," she said in a letter to him, "is that you call me an Englishwoman. I am an Irishwoman," English only through marriage. She told Du Bois that the English denounced her for urging them to clean up their own home before criticizing others. "So while you at one side of the world condemn me for being pro-British, they at the other condemn me for being anti-British." In fact, the book did praise the British people, but it also berated them for not doing enough to eradicate slavery in places under British control.

Du Bois may have been surprised to learn that Lady Simon was not a favorite with British officials. As her husband rose through the government ranks, becoming foreign secretary and chancellor of the exchequer, she met many of them and was harshly criticized by some. One of her husband's colleagues described her as "a good-hearted creature . . . with a tousled Irish head and a great gift for saying the wrong thing. . . . [T]he exterior can only be described as vulgar." To Prime Minister Neville Chamberlain, she was "a sore trial."

But Simon was not out to win any popularity contests. She wanted people to talk about slavery, and they did.

Slow Pace of Change

Changes came to Ethiopia, though not as quickly as Simon would have liked. Italy invaded the African nation in 1935. Six years later, with the Second World War under way, British troops drove Italy out of Ethiopia, and Haile Selassie became emperor. His earlier efforts to wipe out slavery were one reason the British were willing to permit him to return to the throne. Finally, by 1942, the Ethiopian government began enforcing antislavery laws.

The *mui-tsai* system in Hong Kong also came slowly to an end. A strong law passed by the British in 1938 prohibited the system, but the Japanese occupation of the island during the Second World War delayed its enforcement. In 1956, the year after Kathleen Simon's death, the Hong Kong government announced that no new cases of *mui-tsai* had come to light. However, the announcement was premature. Later that year, officials learned of one new *mui-tsai*, but she was the last one known.

Kathleen Simon did not end slavery for all time and in all places, but it was not for want of trying. Her obituary in the London *Times* spoke eloquently of her efforts: "It is hardly an exaggeration to say that she filled the place in Britain that Harriet Beecher Stowe had earlier filled in the United States." Whether people liked her or not, they noticed her, and many fought slavery because of her.

A frequent hiker on St. Paul Island, Alaska, Fredericka Martin learned to keep an eye out for hard, sharp rocks and cinder clumps hidden beneath lush flowers and grass.

CHAPTER 9

"We Have a Lot of
Social Problems Here"

Fredericka Martin

FREDERICKA MARTIN HAD BEEN on the Alaskan island of St. Paul only a short time when she realized something was terribly wrong. "I couldn't stay here all winter," one of the cooks told her, "with hungry kids coming round for dry bread and hawk eyes watching from the office to be sure I didn't give them a crust."

That was the first inkling Martin had that the U.S. government wasn't treating the native population well. The "hungry kids" were the children of the Pribilof Aleuts, native people who spent the summer harvesting fur seals for the U.S. government and living under government control year-round.

Martin and her husband, Samuel Berenberg, had come to St. Paul Island in June 1941, a month after the federal government offered him a job as resident physician on the remote island in the Bering Sea, about 300 miles (480 kilometers) west of the Alaska mainland. They had traveled more than 4,000 miles (6,400 kilometers) from their home in Greenbelt, Maryland.

Their friends were surprised that they agreed to go. They were expecting their first child and would be in an isolated outpost without a modern hospital. Although Berenberg was a doctor and Martin a registered nurse, there would be no obstetrician anywhere nearby. But Martin and Berenberg relished the adventure. She planned on helping her husband in his work, even though she would not be paid. She would also explore the land, meet its people and take care of her baby.

Her plans did not include becoming an advocate for the Aleut people, but that became a passion as soon as she learned how they were being treated. Martin would spend only twelve months on St. Paul, but her active support for its people would last more than ten years and put her in conflict with some of the highest officials in the U.S. government.

Island History

St. Paul Island is the largest of the five Pribilof Islands. When Martin and Berenberg traveled there, Alaska was still a U.S. territory, not a state, and the Pribilof people were wards of the government. St. Paul and St. George, another of the islands, had been prized since 1786, when the Russian navigator Gerasim Pribilof (also written as Gavriil Pribylov) discovered masses of fur seals on the beaches. No one was living on the islands when the Russians arrived and claimed them for their country. The Russians weren't interested in settling the land; they wanted the fur seals' valuable pelts.

But the Russians were not as adept at seal hunting as the native people who came from the Aleutian Islands, about 240 miles (386 kilometers) south of the Pribilofs. So the Russians put them to work. They forced many Aleuts from their homes, relocating them to the Pribilof Islands during the seal harvest in the summer. The Russians were tough taskmasters, and they insisted the Aleuts do the work they demanded and live where they told them to.

By 1820, many of the Aleuts were living year-round on St. Paul and had adopted Russian ways. They spoke a mix of Russian and their native language, attended the Russian Orthodox church and celebrated Russian holidays. The United States acquired the Pribilof Islands as part of their purchase of Alaska from Russia in 1867.

For close to two hundred years, coats made from the pelts of fur seals were the height of fashion in Europe and America. The Pribilof men were the mainstay of the industry, herding the seals, killing them, removing the skins and tanning the hides—all while being underpaid for their work.

Living in Actual Slavery

After the Alaska Purchase, private companies at first ran the fur trade, but in 1910 the U.S. government took full control. It sent federal workers to the islands to oversee the sealing operations and the treatment of the native population. To maintain total control of the labor force, the government forbade the use of the Aleut and Russian languages in island schools and restricted where the Pribilof Aleut people could live, what work they could perform and where they could travel. No one could leave the islands without the permission of a U.S. government official.

By law, the Pribilof Aleut men were to kill seals for the government. The workers performed other tasks during the year too, such as carpentry, plumbing and construction—all in support of the seal industry. For all they did, they rarely received paychecks. Instead of money, the government doled out housing, fuel, food, schooling and medical care. The Aleuts lived in drafty, poorly heated houses without running water. The government rationed food, rarely giving the people meat, fresh vegetables and fruit, or milk. Instruction in school was in English, a language the children didn't speak at home.

Some of the government agents sent to work among the Pribilof Aleuts were appalled. In 1916, one agent told officials in Washington that "the fact cannot be denied that the people of St. Paul (and St. George as well) are living in actual slavery and that this condition exists and is maintained under the immediate control and direction of the United States government."

Martin's Arrival

Little had changed in St. Paul when Fredericka Martin arrived twenty-five years later. The U.S. government still controlled nearly every aspect of the Pribilof Aleuts' lives. They were denied American citizenship and couldn't vote. St. Paul men performed the jobs the U.S. Fish and Wildlife Service required; there were almost no jobs for women. Supplies were still meager; there was little food available at a canteen the Aleuts had set up, and what was there was expensive. Government officials censored people's mail and prohibited their travel. One man who left the island had to fight to be allowed back. When he finally returned, he led a protest for better food and more pay. As punishment, the government exiled him from the island for years.

The white employees of the Fish and Wildlife Service and the island natives were not allowed to socialize. This wasn't a problem for most of the government workers and their wives, but it was for Martin. She wanted to know the people she was living among, and she didn't judge them by their culture, race or social standing.

Martin had tried to learn as much as she could about the islands and the people before she left Maryland, but little information was available. Even government officials couldn't answer her questions about life in the Pribilof Islands. Once there, she had boundless curiosity about people and places, and wanted nothing more than to investigate, explore and question.

The restrictions on the Aleuts seemed so unfair that it didn't take long for her to become outraged. In a letter to a friend on July 24, 1941, a month after arriving on the island, she wrote:

> We have a lot of social problems here we would like to tackle but are wondering just how to go about some of them. I think we can do no better at present than collect facts and pictures and perhaps not use them until we are away, firstly by presenting them to some of the top boys in Washington and secondly by publication.

She began to study the Aleut language so she could talk to the native people, and she also spoke to the Russian Orthodox priest. She read medical notes left by her husband's predecessors and government records in the library, and she took pictures.

Martin was as interested in the island's natural beauty as she was in the people. In a journal she reported all she saw, heard and thought during her year there. In describing a climb along the rock steps of the rookeries, home to the fur seals in the summer, she wrote, "Coils of purplish reddish lava writhed liquidly from tier to tier in adjacent descents." In her notes of January 12, 1942, she wrote:

> How pleasant life would be here if this sort of weather continued, if only the houses were modernly heated and air conditioned. Or, to begin at the beginning, if they had been intelligently constructed by someone who knew how to combat northern weather and winds, and if the material had been of a better sort, seasoned wood, for instance, instead of green wood that shrank, leaving wide gaps for the wind's easy entrance.

This wealth of information became the book *Before the Storm: A Year in the Pribilof Islands, 1941–1942*, which was published after her death.

Fighting Injustice

Martin had a history of helping others. When she was young, she lived for a time with Episcopal nuns and considered becoming one herself. Instead, she became a nurse, working in hospitals in New York City and advancing through the ranks to supervisor and head nurse. She married Alexander Cohen in 1929, and six years later traveled with him to England to visit his parents. That trip took them on to continental Europe, where she saw the early signs of fascism, a form of absolute government control that was on the rise in the 1930s. She recognized the dangers of a system of government in which the people are denied basic rights.

After she returned to the United States, she separated from Cohen and volunteered with a group of doctors, nurses and others who were buying medical supplies, food and clothing to donate to anti-fascist forces in Spain. She was fundraising for the group, the Medical Bureau to Aid Spanish Democracy, when they asked her to go to Spain as chief nurse and administrator of the hospital division. Years later she remembered wanting to go but feeling unqualified, and telling the group, "Who doesn't want to go to Spain? But I'm not fresh out of surgery. You need someone out of surgery." But the organizers didn't want someone with surgical skills; they wanted someone who could lead, and they insisted she was right for the job. Martin was only thirty-one years old when she went to Spain, but her caring attitude toward the patients and the nurses she supervised made them nickname her "Ma."

In Spain, she organized six hospitals, set up a mobile operating unit, supervised more than fifty nurses and withstood nightly air raids. "But it has not been easy," Martin told a *New York Times* reporter when she came home in 1938. "We not only had to accustom ourselves to continuous attack from the air, but at times had to hold a flashlight over an operating table while the surgeon went on with a case. The lights, of course, were extinguished at the first alarm."

She raised money and recruited volunteers for another year, until the end of the war. Then, in 1939, she accepted a job to establish a hospital in Greenbelt,

Maryland. It was there she met Samuel Berenberg, who became her second husband.

Life on St. Paul

On St. Paul Island, Martin never tired of walking, delighting in the flowers, animals, birds and terrain. She thought the island should be one of the greatest tourist spots in the world. But the beauty sat in sharp contrast to the prejudice and injustice, which she could not abide. Just after her arrival, the government agent told her to treat the natives like "dogs or cattle," she wrote in her journal. This was not Martin's way. She would follow the rules but also her conscience.

If the rules said she could not socialize at the homes of the Aleuts, she wouldn't, but they were welcome in hers and often came to see her baby daughter, Tobyanne. The wives of the Fish and Wildlife Service employees objected when she hired an Aleut woman to help with cooking and cleaning, but she was determined not to spend her time with a dishpan and broom. She realized only later that she had broken an unspoken rule by eating food prepared by natives.

The disregard for Aleut natives even affected their medical care. An epidemic of German measles hit shortly before Martin and Berenberg arrived on the island. The practice during epidemics was for Aleut patients to put themselves in the small local jail. When that became too crowded, the newly sick went to a nearby shack. Those who were recovering were supposed to take care of those who were still ill.

Martin visited the sick with Berenberg one day and nearly cried at what she saw. "Crowded and smoked like fish, the men lay fully clothed on the hard bunks," she wrote. "Official eyebrows rose in amusement when we protested against such squalor. We were crazy newcomers who did not know that the Aleut was indifferent to dirt and discomfort." Martin and Berenberg insisted they be moved to a barracks for proper rest and care. They also cleaned and decorated a dingy, abandoned eight-bed hospital so that ill people would have a more inviting place in which to recover in the future.

Hunger, the problem the summer cook had identified, was always there. The federal government rationed the food, leaving the Pribilof Aleuts with a monotonous selection: no eggs, no fresh fruit, no spices. Nothing that could make a plate attractive or flavorful. There was nothing for a child under two and only cereal for children up to age four. Martin's suspicions that the diet was meager were confirmed when she tried to follow it. She wrote:

> I wanted to test out the diet, to see whether I could eat just what a sealer did and have energy to help Sam in the office, run back and forth to the hospital several times a day, spend two or three hours typing, and enjoy a moderate walk. I planned to limit us to the experiment for a week. One day was enough. Or rather too much. We had to calm our surprised protesting neglected stomachs before we could go to sleep. It was not only the kind of food but the small quantity that ended our test.
>
> I no longer wondered why kids sneaked around the garbage cans and ate some of the filthy refuse.

If she couldn't survive on the diet for a day, she wondered how sealers performed their heavy labor on it, and how hungry and poorly nourished schoolchildren could learn.

Wartime

The United States entered the Second World War in December 1941. Six months later, Japanese bombs came close to the Pribilof Islands, and the U.S. government sent the Aleut natives to an evacuation camp on Funter Bay, Alaska, 1,500 miles (2,400 kilometers) away from their homes. Martin and the baby went back to the U.S. mainland, but Berenberg stayed in Alaska until his replacement could arrive.

If life on St. Paul was poor, on Funter Bay it was dismal, depressing and unsanitary. The evacuees were made to live in an abandoned fish cannery, where they were crammed into a decrepit building with rotted floors, broken windows, poor heating, filthy water and insufficient food. The people from St. George endured similarly miserable living quarters in an abandoned gold mine. Berenberg wrote, "[The] present arrangements are utterly mediaeval & unworthy of U.S.

potentialities." The 290 evacuees from St. Paul lacked laundry, toilet, washing and bathing facilities.

But the stay had one unexpected benefit: it brought the Pribilof Aleut people and the rest of America into contact with one another. With so many men at war, employers in the city of Juneau, just four hours away by boat, were desperate for workers. The Fish and Wildlife Service initially prohibited the natives from leaving the evacuation camp, but some St. Paul men escaped and found work in the city. By September 1942 the government allowed them to leave but discouraged them from doing so. Other Pribilof Aleuts wanted to serve in the army and navy. The Fish and Wildlife Service opposed that as well but lost to the needs of the war.

After the War

The government did bring men back to St. Paul for sealing in the summer of 1943, and the entire population was returned in May 1944. U.S. officials thought life would return to the routines of prewar days, but the evacuees had seen that their living conditions could be better. They saw the way other Americans lived, found jobs to do besides seal hunting and learned about other Alaskan natives who were fighting for equal rights. One of the evacuees joined the Alaska Native Brotherhood, a civil rights group, and organized a branch on St. Paul after his return.

What's more, the Aleuts now had a champion for their cause. On the East Coast of the United States, Fredericka Martin was not about to forget her friends on St. Paul, or her promise to tell the rest of the country about them. After the war, she published a book, *Hunting of the Silver Fleece: Epic of the Fur Seal*, and an article about the fur seal industry and the people who worked in it.

Martin's article, "Wanted: A Pribilof Bill of Rights," borrows its title from the American Constitution. The Bill of Rights—the name given to the first ten amendments to the Constitution—promises all Americans certain basic rights and liberties without government interference. Martin wrote that the Pribilof people did not enjoy these same rights, although they were Americans. The article tells the Pribilof Aleuts' history, from their days under Russian rule to their current life as wards of the United States. It asks, "Is there another locality under the Stars and Stripes where citizens are warned that, if they insist upon leaving their birthplace, they cannot return or resume labor at the only means [they have] of earning a living?"

The article appeals to readers to make up for "three-quarters of a century of neglect" and says the "Pribilof Islands will never be the home of democracy unless the sealers' fellow-citizens help them and maintain, from this time forward, most constant vigilance."

A movement for equal rights for Native Americans was spreading throughout the United States after the Second World War, and the Pribilof Aleuts saw themselves as part of it. Martin told their story before organizations that worked for Native American rights, like the National Congress of American Indians, as well as before groups that worked against slavery, like the United Nations Ad Hoc Committee on Slavery. She wrote to magazines and newspapers, as well as to senators, government officials and the president of the United States. She answered questions from the people on St. Paul and replied to their appeals for help. Once, when a confusing letter came from their lawyers, a Pribilof Aleut leader wrote to Martin for advice. Were the lawyers trying to trick them? No, Martin replied, the government is.

Officials of the Fish and Wildlife Service continued to resist changes for the Pribilof people. Even after Martin told them that a 1924 law made all Native Americans citizens, they insisted that the Pribilof Aleuts were not included.

Martin became well known for helping Alaska natives. In 1948, a leader of one of the first Alaska Native Brotherhood groups asked for her assistance in fighting the government on two bills that would deprive Alaska natives of land.

That same year, the National Congress of American Indians invited Martin to testify about those two bills at a congressional hearing. Before a Senate committee, she delivered a detailed and forceful statement that asked pointedly, "Is the United States in 1948 to be more autocratic, more despotic, and more discriminatory than the Russian Czars?"—who ruled over the Pribilof Aleuts before the United States took ownership of Alaska. "No Russian Czar," she wrote, "even contemplated interfering with native occupancy of Alaska lands."

Martin never forgot that she had gone to Spain to fight oppression, only to find it in her own country when she returned. A 1910 law put too much power in one person's hands, she said in a letter to President Harry Truman, and made officials of the Fish and Wildlife Service "indifferent to the rights and needs of human beings." She asked the president to give the Aleut people "title to their lands and quickly."

Friend of the Aleuts

While she was working for the Aleut people, Martin's own life was changing. Her marriage to Berenberg was coming to an end, and in 1950 she moved with Tobyanne to Mexico. She did not return to nursing but instead worked as a translator, travel writer and teacher at a language institute.

Changes also came to the Aleut people. In 1950 the government enacted a new wage plan, based largely on one Martin had outlined. It wasn't perfect, but it gave the people an annual wage instead of store rations, and it was the first small step toward equal rights. Martin remained in contact with her St. Paul friends, and continued to write letters to newspapers and officials in support of equal rights. But the native people had gained experience and confidence, and no longer depended on her.

The Aleut community on St. Paul Island filed a lawsuit with the Indian Claims Commission, a panel set up by the U.S. Congress in 1946 to hear complaints against the government. The Aleuts claimed that they had exclusive rights to St. Paul and demanded to be compensated fairly for the work they did from 1870, when the federal government declared the Pribilof Islands a "special reservation." That would be a long legal battle, and Martin remained involved, sending letters demanding equal pay and equal rights.

The Fur Seal Act of 1966—which transferred government land and houses to the Aleut people—was one of Martin's successes. Alaska, which had become a state in 1959, would be in charge of education, and the U.S. Public Health Service would be responsible for health care.

Another success came twenty-seven years after the group filed its complaint with the Indian Claims Commission. The commission concluded that the native people of St. Paul Island had been underpaid for more than seventy-six years, and it ordered the government to give them their back pay. More than eight million dollars went to individuals and to the local government for community projects.

In 1986, the people of St. Paul Island declared Martin an honorary citizen, and the University of Alaska awarded her an honorary doctorate. The island became her final resting place in 2007, when her daughter, Tobyanne, brought her ashes there for burial. Her epitaph speaks eloquently of her work:

FREDERICKA I. MARTIN
June 1, 1905–October 4, 1992
An Internationalist who
fought for peace in the
Spanish Civil War and for the
rights of the Aleut People
of the Pribilof Islands.

St. Paul Island may seem an odd location for her plot, since she lived in Mexico for forty-two years before she died. But just a few years before her death, she told an interviewer that when people asked her if her work in Spain was her proudest accomplishment, she always told them she was most proud of the work she did for her Aleut friends.

Canadian Prime Minister Stephen Harper and Diane Finley, Minister of Human Resources and Skills Development, present Timea E. Nagy with the Prime Minister's Volunteer Award for Emerging Leader on December 14, 2012.

CHAPTER 10

"Everyone Is Worth It"

Timea Nagy

TIMEA NAGY GRIPPED THE MICROPHONE. She had never even considered writing a book, but a friend had given her his ticket to a writers' seminar in New York City, and how could you turn down a free trip to Manhattan? Now the conference was winding down, and she had to stand up in front of the group to deliver an "elevator pitch"—the thirty-second sales presentation she would give if she ran into a book publisher on an elevator.

"Then it just came out of me," Nagy remembered in a later interview. "I think what I said was, 'There was a girl who grew up in Hungary. She came to Canada thinking she would work as a nanny. But it wasn't a nanny; she was forced to be a sex slave. But there's a happy ending because she's standing in front of you to tell her story.'"

It was a moment that changed Nagy's life. She'd never told her story in public, and she was afraid people would think she was "filthy" if she did. This audience didn't. Instead, their "jaws dropped and it was quiet, and then some lady started crying, and they clapped and gave me a standing ovation."

A whole new life unfolded for Nagy from the moment she shared her secret with those total strangers in New York. She did write that book, and then she went further: she devoted her life to helping women who'd been tricked into sexual slavery. The organization she founded, Walk With Me Canada Victim Services, now offers round-the-clock emergency care to victims of sex trafficking in Ontario, Canada. Walk With Me also educates law enforcement officers and advocates for stronger anti-trafficking laws. (Human trafficking is defined by the U.S. State Department as "the use of deceit or coercion to force a person to work without pay, often in a new location.")

Coming to Canada

Nagy's story started in Hungary in April 1998. For months, she and her brother had struggled to earn money, and they were in danger of losing their home. Nagy got in touch with an agency that arranged short-term employment in Canada, which soon told her it had found her work as a nanny or cleaner for three months. Nagy was excited. The job in Canada would be her chance to experience a new country and return to Budapest with enough money in her pocket to pay off the debt on the apartment she and her brother owned together.

But when she arrived in Toronto, she wasn't welcomed by employers who took her to their home to care for their children or clean their house. Instead, she was greeted by two Hungarian men and a Canadian who drove her to a strip club. There, her job was to dance in front of men in a suggestive manner. She was sexually assaulted by the club's owner, Alfonzo, and forced to work nineteen-hour days, six days a week. Her Hungarian handlers claimed most of the money she earned for themselves. When she took some of this money to buy herself a sandwich one day, they rebuked her. "You owe us thousands of dollars, and until you pay that off, none of the money that you make is yours," she was told. "Tomorrow you will make an extra fifty dollars as a penalty."

Alfonzo even sent her one day to a massage parlor he owned, where she was expected to work as a prostitute. But Nagy did not dare attempt to escape. Like many trafficked women, she didn't know a word of English when she arrived and didn't know where she was. And she was scared. She didn't trust her handlers, who she later learned were two of the most notorious traffickers of Hungarian women in Canada, but she also didn't trust the Canadian police. Her handlers had told her the police would throw her in jail for working illegally. The Hungarians also threatened to harm her family back in Hungary if she didn't cooperate with them. Years later she explained, "Anyone who questions my motives, or the motives of any woman placed in this impossible position, does so ignorant of a woman's protective instinct toward her family."

Her handlers soon began driving her to work at a fancier strip club, and as her time there continued, she was able to watch the two men carefully. Though traumatized by all she had suffered, she came to realize that they were not watching her every move, especially as they weren't welcome inside the new club.

She already had a return plane ticket (which Canada required of anyone on a temporary work permit) and a passport under a false name. Now, determined to escape, she sought help from sympathetic people working at the club—a DJ and one of the dancers. They helped her find places to live where her handlers couldn't find her while she earned some money dancing, and she was able to catch her return flight to Hungary—but not to safety.

When she told her story to the Hungarian police, they sexually assaulted her instead of protecting her. At the same time, her Hungarian traffickers returned to Budapest, where they intimidated her by staking out her apartment to keep her from testifying against them in court.

Return to Canada

Once again, she had to escape, and the only place she could think to go was Canada. Using money she'd earned behind her handlers' backs, she bought her own plane ticket and entered the country as a tourist. She moved in with a woman who had befriended her at the club. A tourist visa would let Nagy stay in Canada for six months, but it meant she could not legally work to earn money. But Nagy had no choice; she needed money to survive. She had to find a job that paid her "under the table," which meant it was illegal. She got a job dancing at a club, but soon graduated to bartending, work that was less devastating to her self-esteem but was still illegal.

One day, her housemate showed Nagy a newspaper article: Canadian police had set up a task force to curb the trafficking of Eastern European women like her. This might be the chance she was hoping for to stay in Canada, she thought. She promptly tracked down the Hungarian police translator named in the article, and he accompanied her to the headquarters of the Royal Canadian Mounted Police (known in Canada as the Mounties). For the next eight hours, two detectives listened to her story. Her evidence, they assured her, would help them bring Alfonzo, the club owner, to justice on charges of sexual assault. Nagy was in Canada illegally, but the Mounties would help her stay while the case worked its way through the courts, and the danger she faced back in Hungary strengthened her claim that she was a genuine refugee.

Six years passed between Alfonzo's arrest and his trial, and because sexual assault is difficult to prove, he was ultimately not convicted. But Nagy made an impressive witness. After the trial, Alfonzo's defense attorney told her she was "by far the toughest witness I've ever dealt with."

Nagy was grateful to the detectives who had guided her through the immigration hearing and trial, and she wanted to show them that they'd made the right decision in trusting her. "I dreamed I'd one day make them proud," she said.

Once she could work legally, she made a living at jobs like hairdressing and waitressing. But she was looking for something more and began to volunteer for a crisis hotline. The organization that ran this service offered its volunteers training in trauma counseling. That's when Nagy discovered a talent she hadn't suspected: "I was able to connect with, understand and support people in unfortunate and difficult situations." She began to hone the skills she would use three years later, after she spoke publicly of her own trauma in New York.

Courage to Speak Out

When she returned to her seat after her elevator pitch at the writers' conference, Nagy felt a tap on her shoulder. The stranger identified himself as Jeff Lanza, a retired FBI agent. "I'm doing training on human trafficking," he explained, "but I've never met a victim who would tell her story. Would you come and present with me?"

Nagy had never told anyone her full story before, but she felt ready now. A woman who'd been at the writing seminar ran a small publishing house in Vancouver, Canada. She invited Nagy and Lanza to meet there to discuss publishing a book about Nagy's experiences. That book became *Memoirs of a Sex Slave Survivor*.

This happened in 2009, the year before Vancouver hosted the Winter Olympics; Nagy began to contact people who work with victims of trafficking and warn them of a likely spike in activity for this international event. One of these contacts introduced her to Benjamin Perrin, a law professor at the University of British Columbia and a world expert on human trafficking. "We talked for two hours," Nagy later recalled, "and he asked me, straight out, 'What are you going to do now, now that you see what's wrong?' And I looked at him and I said, 'Hmmm. I want to tell my stories to the police so they know how to find the victims. I want to help the police.'" Perrin said that because of his many contacts in law enforcement, he could help her with that. "I will send an email to the [Mounties]," he told her. "I will send an email to the Toronto police and other police agencies I work with."

By the time Nagy got back to Toronto from Vancouver, she had speaking invitations from the Mounties and the Toronto police, and "after that it just snowballed." She began a new career training law-enforcement officers. The Mounties sent her on a cross-country speaking tour, from British Columbia on the west coast to Nova Scotia on the east.

Because of her personal experience as a victim of international trafficking, Nagy had insights that government officials who were drafting new anti-trafficking laws didn't have. Joy Smith, a member of Parliament, called on Nagy for help when she sponsored a bill to prosecute Canadians and permanent residents who commit trafficking offenses outside the country. At Smith's request, Nagy addressed a parliamentary committee about trafficking. The bill passed.

Once Nagy began giving seminars to police, they started asking, "Can we call you if we have a victim? Can you talk to the victim?" Increasingly, when someone refused to speak with the police, they would call her. Nagy would meet with the young woman, take her to a hotel, feed her and care for her. Police force after police force sought her out—"It just never stopped," she remembered. She earned some income by working at a shelter in 2009, but by 2010 she had to quit. She was with victims nonstop, which was draining and exhausting, and she had no money from anyone to support her work. "I just did it from my pocket—all of it. I just drove like a maniac, left, right, and center. I drove 280,000 kilometers [174,000 miles] in eighteen months—Montreal, Ottawa, Windsor. In 2010, from January till August, I worked about 320 hours a month. There were times when I didn't sleep for three days."

This was critical work that no one else was doing. Without realizing it, Nagy was single-handedly doing all the work of a nonprofit organization. "All I knew was that I didn't want to go to work in the shelter anymore," she recalled. "I wanted to go and pick up victims . . . and assist law enforcement. But I had no idea you had to call it an agency and collect donations and have a website and email addresses. That was still all new to me; I was just a girl with a suitcase."

Walk With Me

Around this time, Nagy began to give talks to raise public awareness of trafficking in Canada. Robert Hooper and his wife, Jill Trites, heard her speak. "She is such an effective speaker," Hooper, a lawyer, remembered, that she "has the ability to make grown men cry." With a seventeen-year-old daughter at home, the couple could sympathize keenly with the girls Nagy was helping. But because of his experience with other community agencies, Hooper understood that her efforts needed more structure, and he stepped in. He provided an office for her at his law firm in Hamilton, Ontario. He found her an administrative assistant and did the legal work necessary to get a nonprofit agency off the ground, and Walk With Me Victim Services was born. Trites is now the organization's executive director, and Hooper is the chair.

Walk With Me started small, but it has grown enormously in only a few years. It has three front-line staff—all survivors of sex trafficking—on call twenty-four hours a day, seven days a week. Volunteers bring meals to survivors and take them to medical appointments. The organization works, Nagy said, because survivors help survivors.

> I think I gain their trust immediately when I say I've been beaten, I've been raped, I left my family behind, I've been in court just like you will be. So it's not someone who can't imagine how you feel and is reading something from a textbook. Sometimes they ask me, "Why are you here at 3 a.m.? You don't even know me. Why are you trying to help me?" And I say, "Because everyone is worth it, even though you may not think you're worth it at this moment. And I was you fifteen years ago."

The moment the police phone the Walk With Me office to say that a woman has been rescued from sex slavery, staff members spring into action. A volunteer meets the victim at the police station and, if the victim decides to come with her, takes her to a safe house where she can sleep, eat and just relax for three days. Walk With Me secured funding for the house in 2011; it has four private bedrooms, two bathrooms, a laundry and a large kitchen. Victims with children are welcome, and so are pets. A security system, with no Internet or phone access, guarantees safety.

Walk With Me also provides emergency financial support, including gift cards for food and clothing, dental and medical care, translation help for victims who don't speak English and immigration and legal assistance. It even offers money for tattoo removal, since traffickers sometimes humiliate their victims by branding them as their "property." Although Walk With Me doesn't offer long-term rehabilitation, it does refer victims to other outreach services that will help with psychological and job counseling.

The organization followed up on the fifty-five victims, both women and men, it had helped in 2012. According to their annual report for that year, all had broken their ties with their traffickers, and most had gone back to school, found jobs or reunited with their families. Many of the victims also went to court to testify against their traffickers.

Walk With Me believes education can help prevent and reduce trafficking. Since 2009, Nagy has worked with or trained thousands of law-enforcement personnel in Canada. American judges and Canadian attorneys general have attended her sessions. Her booklet *Mindset of a Human Trafficking Victim: First Aid Guide for Service Providers* teaches police and other front-line workers how to treat victims with sensitivity; it explains how traffickers gain control of the girls' minds and highlights the threats, intimidation and brainwashing the victims endure.

Pimps and traffickers target teenagers and young women who appear vulnerable. To raise awareness among these potential victims, Walk With Me offers resources for high school students and teachers, youth workers and group home workers. In its free tool kit, young victims tell their stories in order to warn the most at-risk youngsters about the men who would exploit them.

In one typical exchange, a victim explains why she was susceptible to a pimp's attention. "Unfortunately, around the age of fifteen, my parents weren't doing the best," she says. "Suddenly I felt that instead of being needed and wanted, I was alone." Then a pimp describes how he zeros in on that vulnerability: "You identify each girl's weakness, [so] you can tap into that specific spot, where it's like, 'You don't feel like anybody gets you. I'm going to listen to you the best.'"

Walk With Me runs at least two fund-raisers a year—a Freedom Walk (sponsored jointly with Free Them, another anti-trafficking organization) and the

Journey to Freedom Gala. With more money, Nagy would be able to expand her services. Currently, Walk With Me's focus is on emergency help, but Nagy would like to offer long-term rehabilitation and a longer-term safe house. Of course, what she would really like is to end trafficking altogether, but she believes only stiffer sentences will deter the criminals. She sees a need for a twenty-year minimum sentence.

Human trafficking is what Nagy calls a "ghost crime"—a crime that is "designed not to be seen"—since many victims are so brainwashed and intimidated that they refuse to testify in court. As a result, it is hard to estimate the number of trafficking victims in her adopted country, but Nagy believes it is a much bigger problem than the public recognizes. From 2009 to early 2013, Walk With Me took more than six hundred calls from police and social service agencies, and directly helped almost three hundred victims.

In the summer of 2014, Nagy and Robert Hooper represented Walk With Me before a committee of Canada's Parliament. The government was holding hearings on a new bill that would radically change the country's prostitution laws. It would now be illegal to purchase sex, while in most cases prostitutes would not be charged with any crime. To make the case for the new law, Nagy told her own story, hoping to convince members of Parliament that "prostitution is not a profession. It's an oppression." Once prostitutes are assured that they have committed no crime, Nagy believes more of them will feel free to approach police for help in escaping their degrading and unsafe lives.

For her work, Nagy has been recognized with an array of awards, including the Prime Minister's Volunteer Award for Emerging Leader, the Queen Elizabeth II Diamond Jubilee Medal and the Frederick Douglass Award from the American antislavery organization Free the Slaves.

After Nagy escaped from slavery, her self-esteem was shattered. She felt guilty for accepting a vague job offer in Canada. Even when she said yes to the offer, she explains in her memoir, "Deep inside, I knew something was weird. I didn't listen to my instinct. I went against it and I lost." It took her years to stop blaming herself and to regain her self-respect. Now Nagy believes that the women she works with can do what she did. She says:

There is no such thing as too damaged—it's just a matter of if she's ready—ready to go on a healing journey. You can be extremely damaged to the point where people would look at you and say, "Why would she even bother to get up? She may as well just roll over and die because she's never going to get over it." But then that person will get up on her own and, against all odds, will turn her life around only because she wanted to and she was ready to face all her demons. And it's not our job to decide that she needs to heal or she can't be healed; that's not for us to judge.

Nagy named her agency Walk With Me because the organization accompanies its clients on their way to rebuilding their lives. "I don't take them for a walk," she explains. "They're the boss."

Micheline Slattery speaks at the University of South Carolina Aiken in 2008.

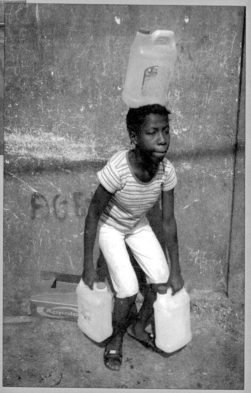

A fourteen-year-old *restavec* in Haiti performs arduous work for the family that bought her.

CHAPTER 11

"The Best Way to Remove Shame Is to Expose the Shame"

Micheline Slattery

MICHELINE SLATTERY RADIATES SELF-ASSURANCE with her beaming smile, ready laugh, elegant style and relaxed manner. But she was not always so confident. For years, she lived in shame, fearful of admitting who she was. "I was always living a lie," Slattery said in an interview. "I used to pretend I was Jamaican because I didn't want anyone to know I was Haitian. I never mingled with anyone who was Haitian, just so I could put that life behind me." By "that life," Slattery meant her nine years of enslavement in Haiti and four years of enslavement in the United States.

When she was eighteen years old, Slattery escaped from slavery, but another ten years passed before she began to speak openly about her painful history. In March 2004, a therapist suggested that she talk about her experiences, and that very month she told her story to thousands of people who'd tuned in to a public radio interview. Many of them wrote or called afterward, praising her and saying they were shocked to learn that slavery could occur in the United States. Later that month, she repeated her story to a large audience at an International Women's Day event in Boston.

The more Slattery talked, the easier it became for her to grapple with her years as a child slave. And the more she talked, the more people realized that slavery still exists, and many asked how they could help.

Childhood in Haiti

Slattery's story begins in Haiti in 1982, when she was five years old. Her mother had just died, leaving her an orphan. Later, when she was much older, she learned that her mother had been killed by the Tonton Macoute, a private police force working for the Haitian dictator Jean-Claude Duvalier. The same group had killed her father when she was an infant. At five, Micheline was too young to understand and too busy even to wonder what happened after her mother's last good-bye kiss.

Micheline's aunt Jocelyne took her into her home, but not to love as a niece. The child was to be her *restavec*, a word derived from the French *reste avec*, meaning "staying with." The idea of children staying with relatives sounds innocent, but there was nothing innocent about it for Micheline. A *restavec* is a slave in everything but name. A *restavec* works but does not get paid, cannot quit and can be sold.

Micheline became a slave to Jocelyne, her husband and their ten children—someone to make beds, wash dishes, mop floors, dust furniture and launder clothes. The home had no plumbing, so each morning at dawn Micheline walked to a lake to fill buckets with water and carry the heavy load back to the house. This morning trek, alone and across snake-infested grasses, was the first of several she made for water each day. When she was five, she carried about a gallon (almost 4 liters) on each trip, but as she got older, she carried as much as 6 gallons (23 liters) at a time. In each hand she held one or two buckets, and she carried two more suspended from a rope across her neck. No one listening to Slattery's story would fault her for sounding resentful about this arduous chore, but there was no bitterness in her voice as she described it. Instead she joked, "That's probably why I have such good posture now."

Micheline traveled the same route each day, with a wicker basket filled with clothes, to do the laundry by hand in the lake. Today, as a grown woman, she remembers the hours she spent doing the wash as the only peaceful time she had to think about her mother. Back in the house, if Micheline did anything Jocelyne did not like—forgot to refill the water buckets, failed to finish her chores on time, moved too slowly—her aunt would whip her with a flexible rod made specifically for the purpose.

The practice of taking in children as *restavecs* is common in Haiti. "Many families have a little maid," Slattery explained in an interview. "These children don't have a life of their own." The young Slattery had no time for play, no time for learning and no time to talk to anyone but herself. She was at the beck and call of everyone in the house—even the other children, who were as free with their orders as the adults.

Micheline often lived for several months at a time with two other cousins in Haiti, Thérèse and Léonie. At Thérèse's home, she did much the same work as she did for Jocelyne, but she had an even more terrifying time. There she was raped, and Thérèse attacked her with a knife for mentioning it.

At Léonie's, Micheline enjoyed a brief taste of kindness. Léonie was married but had no children of her own. When her young cousin arrived, Léonie bought her clothes, gave her a pretty room and sent her to a prestigious private school for about a year. Then Léonie became pregnant and lost all interest in Micheline. Léonie withdrew her from the good school and moved her from the house into a shack, and Micheline's life as a *restavec* resumed.

Childhood in America

When Micheline was fourteen years old, Léonie again gave her reason to hope that her life would improve. She sent her to America, where the child thought dreams come true. For three weeks, she was happy. She lived with a half sister in Miami, and they spent their days shopping, talking and taking orders from no one. Then Léonie arrived, and all of Micheline's illusions were shattered. Her cousin told her she was to be a *restavec* for a cousin she did not know who lived in Connecticut. Léonie was a human trafficker, a person who was paid for transporting children into slavery in the United States. Micheline was one of those children.

In December of that year, Léonie sent Micheline to New York, and at the airport she was met by her cousin Marielina. "That's one of the moments I'll never forget—when that stranger picked me up," Slattery later said, her voice touched with sorrow, as if she was reliving all the pain of her life with Marielina. Though her days in Haiti had been demanding and joyless, they were also familiar: she knew the people, the language and the land. In Connecticut she knew no one and nothing—not the language, not the streets and not the gray, wintery sky. Slattery remembers her first days in Connecticut as a time of bright Christmas lights, a biting chill in the air—and an overwhelming feeling of sadness.

Marielina, her husband and their three young children lived in a small apartment. (There would be another baby about a year later.) Micheline had the living room couch for a bed and no room of her own. Her workday began early in the morning, when she woke up the young children, who greeted her with kicks, slaps and bites. She dressed them, fed them and took them to school before she could even think of her own school day ahead. She was nanny, maid, laundress and cook—the family's unpaid drudge—as well as a schoolgirl.

Micheline attended a middle school, but she was late so often—with so much to do before she could leave the house—that the principal regularly called Marielina about her tardiness. Her cousin said the girl was lazy and overslept, no matter how hard Marielina tried to get her up. Micheline bristled as she listened to the lie, but she was too afraid to tell the principal the truth. She herself made excuses for Marielina when her teachers asked her why her cousin didn't attend parents' night. Micheline could never forget Marielina's warning that if the teachers at school found out the truth, she would be sent back to Haiti, where Léonie would attack her with a machete.

Throughout middle school and high school, Micheline felt like an outsider, someone who belonged not to the family she lived with or any of the crowds at school. She knew no English when she arrived, and dressed in long skirts from a secondhand store, she looked so different from the other students. Her classmates either teased her or ignored her. "[But] I didn't have time to be lonely," she recalled. "I was too busy. By the time I lay down on the couch at night, I was gone." She never thought of confiding her troubles to anyone—teachers or students—because she was too frightened and ashamed. "The shame was always there."

She remembers learning in her U.S. history classes about the Civil War and realizing that she was just like the slaves. "I was doing everything they did. The only difference is that I'm not in the past," she said. "I was living in a free country, and other people were living the old ways—owning slaves. I felt humiliation and shame."

She always hoped for a kind word from Marielina but was always disappointed. "She would call me a 'dirty dog' and would twist my ear to the point that it would bleed," Slattery remembered. But Marielina never beat her with a belt for fear it would leave a mark, and she was always careful not to let strangers see that she had mistreated her.

One day Micheline asked her, "If you don't like me, why don't you send me back to Haiti?" Marielina said it was because she had paid $2,500 for her. For a long time, Slattery thought that was what she was worth—that her value could be calculated in dollars and cents.

Micheline attended church regularly, but even there, she did not become friends with the other kids. She did develop an abiding faith in God and a fervent belief that he has a reason for all he does. Because of her faith, Slattery was able to express some gratitude toward Marielina. "She gave me one gift that no amount of money can purchase, a gift that no one can take away from me: my relationship with God. If it hadn't been for her, I would not have my belief."

Moving On

When Micheline Slattery was seventeen years old, Marielina added to her workload by forcing her to get a job outside the home. She found work as a cashier at a chain restaurant nearby. She worked six days a week, while continuing to look after Marielina's children and attend school. On a typical weekday, she would pick up the children after school, make sure they had supper, get to the restaurant by five o'clock and work until eleven. "If I was lucky, I would get five hours of sleep," she said. In spite of her long hours, her job was a restful escape from some of the pressures of home. Marielina took her paychecks at first, but Slattery soon learned from the other employees that she could open a bank account of her own. As the weeks passed, she saved some money, taking her first small step toward independence.

At eighteen, she was legally an adult and old enough to be on her own. She moved out of her cousin's home and rented a one-room apartment in an elderly neighbor's home. Marielina tried many times to get her to move back, but Slattery was not about to give up her first taste of freedom. "She tried to threaten me, and she said [that] I was going to die, that I was going to get AIDS," Slattery said. It can be frightening to be on your own after years of following orders, but Slattery never considered going back.

She began to live on her own terms, making friends and connecting with her brother, who had also been a *restavec*, as well as with her half sister and half brother. She moved to Massachusetts and began nursing school, working part-time as a nursing assistant while studying. Though her early school years had been miserable in so many ways, the school was generous in providing her with a Haitian tutor, Slattery says. This served her well in pursuing nursing school and her chosen profession. "I believe that you need a job so you can do right by yourself," she explained.

Though life was better than ever, some days a cloud seemed to descend over Slattery. "I would be sitting and talking to you," she said, "and then my expression would change. I would be somewhere else." The past would well up inside her, and the sadness of her childhood—from her mother's death up until her escape to the neighbor's apartment—would overwhelm her. "I never felt free because I was reliving those things over and over."

When she was twenty-nine years old, Slattery went to a therapist for help. Until then, she had never told her whole story to anyone. "There is such a taboo against talking about *restavecs* in Haiti," she explained. "But I learned [that] the best way to remove shame is to expose the shame."

Speaking Out

Before her speech at the International Women's Day event in Boston, Slattery was so nervous that she could not sit still. She turned restlessly in her seat looking for Shawnee Hunt, the woman who would introduce her. Slattery had never met her and expected her to be intimidating, but she turned out to be the friendly woman seated next to her. Hunt had been the U.S. ambassador to Austria and was accustomed to public speaking, while Slattery was a former slave who'd spent years shying away from talking about herself. She could not imagine how she would follow such an experienced speaker to the podium. But when Hunt called her name, Slattery rose with speech in hand, focused her attention on one person in the audience to calm herself and told her story. The response was powerful; people had not known that slavery still existed in the world, certainly not in the United States.

Slattery decided that she had to continue to speak out, both for her own sake and for the sake of those still enslaved in Haiti and the United States. Since her first speech, audiences have heard her on college campuses, at high schools and at conferences. At a social work meeting in Connecticut, public officials were embarrassed to learn that slavery was being practiced in their own state. "I think they were appalled that I grew up there and this happened there," she said.

People frequently ask Slattery about taking Marielina to court, but she has decided to leave any punishment in God's hands. "The Lord always repays you," she said. When she saw her at a family funeral, her cousin asked for money for gasoline and Slattery gave it to her.

Slattery's interest is not in punishing people for the past but in helping people toward a good future. The goal of her speeches is to encourage people to end the *restavec* system.

Haiti was one of the first nations to prohibit slavery, in 1804, but the country allows *restavecs* to this day. Recent laws passed there do require that children go to school and be treated humanely, but those laws are often not enforced. Haitians who come to the United States bring their traditions with them, and one of those traditions is owning a *restavec*. As Americans learn about the practice, Slattery hopes Haitians will be shamed into ending it.

Slattery would also like people to be alert to the signs of slavery. "In any home, if there is a foreigner, older or younger—a person who is always around, who always seems to be doing the housework and running after the children, who doesn't seem to belong, who doesn't have a life of her own—that is one of the signs," she said. Slaves are likely to live in fear and with shame, as Slattery did. They are not likely to seek help. If teachers, police and social workers know the signs, they can encourage both *restavecs* and adult slaves to talk honestly.

Slattery has not returned to Haiti since Léonie sent her away when she was fourteen, and she has no interest in going there. She is enjoying being a mother to a young son and said life is good for her now. Her interest is in helping to make it good for others.

Hadijatou Mani with her baby in April 2008, six months before her anti-slavery lawsuit against Niger is decided.

CHAPTER 12

"I Was Sold Like a Goat"

Hadijatou Mani

HADIJATOU MANI STEPPED FORWARD SHYLY to receive an International Woman of Courage Award. Michelle Obama, the wife of President Barack Obama, put her arm around her and ushered her toward Hillary Clinton, the secretary of state. Mani's head was slightly bowed during the ceremony, which was in English, a language she could not understand. Though timid and reserved, she had found inner strength and a powerful voice when she fought for freedom from slavery in the African nation of Niger. Mani earned the award by taking her country's government to court, thereby easing the way for other slaves.

Praise and recognition were new to Mani. For most of her twenty-four years, she'd received scorn, not honor. But her life changed dramatically when she gained her freedom on October 27, 2008. By March 11, 2009—the day she received her award in Washington, DC—she had, for the first time, testified in court, boarded a plane, traveled outside her country, felt the chill of a cold winter's day and enjoyed freedom without fear that she would be forced back into slavery.

Born into Slavery

Because Mani was the daughter of a slave, she was born into slavery in Niger, a poor, hot, dry and dusty country in West Africa. In 1996, when she was twelve, Mani was sold to a prominent man of forty-six, Souleymane Naroua, for more money than most people in Niger earned in a year. "I was sold like a goat," she later said.

Mani became a *sadaka*—literally "a fifth wife"—to Naroua. But a *sadaka* has little in common with a traditional wife. She is not married to the man she's bound to and has none of the rights or privileges of a lawful wife. She is the man's possession—compelled to work in his house and fields; to be a concubine, giving her owner sexual pleasure; and to obey the master in all things. Naroua had seven other *sadakas*, as well as the four wives he was allowed under Islamic tradition.

From the time she became Naroua's *sadaka*, Mani had to work every day, without pay, without vacations and without respect. She suffered so much under Naroua's cruel beatings and insults that she ran away often—so many times that she gave up counting. Each time, Naroua would drag her back and humiliate her. He once left her practically naked in a public area, where anyone could see her. His cruelty continued in spite of the fact that she had two living children by him and two others who died in infancy.

A New Law

Mani was unaware that there were people fighting to set her free. In Niger, the nonprofit organization Timidria (a word that means "solidarity" in one of the country's local languages) had been struggling to make slavery illegal since 1991, and other antislavery organizations were at work around the world. One of them, Anti-Slavery International, based in England, cooperated closely with Timidria. Under pressure from these antislavery groups, as well as foreign governments, Niger passed a law on May 5, 2003, that made slavery a crime punishable by a fine and up to thirty years in jail. But although the law was on the books, authorities did not enforce it, and Mani remained a slave.

News travels slowly in Niger, where few people have access to TV, radio and the Internet. If no one told a slave she was free, she would not know—and slave owners usually said nothing. Timidria turned its attention to spreading the word and freeing the slaves.

Timidria staff members traveled throughout the country, to the cities and the remote areas, and one day in 2005, someone arrived at Naroua's home. "The representative from Timidria was very clear," said Romana Cacchioli, program and advocacy team manager of Anti-Slavery International. "He told Naroua, 'Look, we're aware that you have these slave girls. You need to release them; you need to free them. And if you don't we will prosecute you according to the law, and we won't hesitate to see you're convicted.'"

On August 18, 2005, two years after the law to end slavery in Niger was passed, Naroua presented Mani with a certificate of release. Still, he would not let her go. He claimed that when she ceased being his slave, she automatically became his wife. But Mani did not want to be his wife, his slave or a member of his household in any way. He had terrorized her for years, and now she wanted to live as she chose.

Mani finally gained her release when a man from Timidria met her brother in a marketplace and learned that she was still at Naroua's. With the help of the two men, she escaped.

In the Courts of Niger

Afraid that Naroua would try to bring her back to his home, as he had so many times before, Mani went to court with the help of Timidria, Anti-Slavery International and a local lawyer. She told the judge that her former master was not letting her live the way she wanted, even though he had freed her. In his decision, the judge said Mani "was free to start her life all over with any person of her own choice," because there had been no official wedding binding her to Naroua. None of the requirements for a legal marriage had been met—no consent by Mani, no payment of a dowry (a present from the bride's family to the groom's at the time of a marriage), no religious ceremony and no broken and shared kola nut (traditional at weddings in the region).

Naroua refused to accept the decision and appealed to the family court. This court reached a different conclusion, ruling that under Niger's customary law, which takes into account both tradition and written laws, a slave girl automatically becomes her owner's wife after she is freed. According to that court, Mani was married to Naroua and had to live with him.

Mani appealed the decision, still hoping to gain her right to freedom through the courts of Niger. In the meantime, she had fallen in love with a man named Lada Rabo. They had married with her brother's consent, and she was pregnant with their child. Naroua complained to the police about Mani's marriage, and she was charged with bigamy (entering into a marriage with one person when you're already legally married to another). Mani, Rabo and her brother, who had been a witness to their marriage, were each sentenced to six months in jail. "She was absolutely petrified for herself and her unborn child," said Romana Cacchioli.

Mani appealed that decision. After two months, the court suspended her sentence and released her from jail, pending the outcome of the family court appeal.

In the ECOWAS Court

Mani was fighting two legal cases simultaneously: she was appealing the finding that she was Naroua's wife and awaiting a decision on the charge of bigamy.

The courts were all ignoring the question of slavery, but slavery was central to the issue of whether Mani and Naroua were married. He could claim that Mani was his wife only because the family court had deemed slavery acceptable under customary law.

Mani's team was not optimistic about these proceedings in Niger's courts. Naroua often bragged that he had the ear of the country's president, and he already had two victories. "We felt we had to force the state of Niger to recognize the issue of slavery," said Cacchioli. They decided to take the case to the Economic Community of West African States (ECOWAS) Community Court of Justice, the regional court for most West African nations. One of the responsibilities of the ECOWAS court is to hear cases dealing with violations of human rights. Now Mani's case was not against Naroua but against the state of Niger. She claimed that the country had violated her human rights by failing to protect her from slavery and discrimination against women.

The ECOWAS court was still new in 2007, Cacchioli said. It had not heard many human rights cases and had never before heard a slavery case. Mani's lawyers were not even sure if they could call her as a witness, but they did.

The courtroom was packed. The seven justices were there, TV cameras were running and all eyes were on Hadijatou Mani as she began to tell her story. She was nervous. "When you're a slave girl and you've been told all your life that you're nothing, your fear is that no one will believe you," Cacchioli explained. Now, she was about to speak to educated people, although she herself had no education.

"'You just tell your story,' we told her," Cacchioli said. "Two of the justices were women, so we told her those judges were just like us. They want to hear your story directly from you. Tell it to them the way you told it to us." Fearful as she was, Mani drew courage from knowing that if she won the case, she would save her children from suffering as she had. Even more, she wanted to secure a future for her family. Once, everything she had—even her clothes and her body—belonged to her master, Naroua, but she dreamed of owning a small farm to provide a livelihood for the present and something to pass on to her loved ones for the future. As she waited, she worried that this was an impossible dream.

The official language of the court was French, but Mani speaks a variation of Hausa, a native language, so the court provided translators. Luckily, one justice understood Hausa and noticed errors in the translation. The court would have to find a new interpreter who could translate accurately, and that would take hours. Mani's long wait to testify became even longer.

The next day she had her chance, and when she spoke, "the court was transfixed," Cacchioli said. There were gasps as she described her treatment over a dozen years. Slavery in Niger was no secret, but no one before had spoken about it so openly, and certainly no one had ever had the courage to accuse the state of Niger of a crime by failing to protect her from enslavement. "It was very difficult to challenge my former master and to speak out when people see you as nothing more than a slave," Mani said after the trial in a written statement issued by Anti-Slavery International. "But I knew that this was the only way to protect my child from suffering the same fate as myself."

From the moment she began to give her evidence, Mani was elated. She had never before felt that anyone wanted to listen to her, but here were dignitaries who had traveled from outside the country just to hear her story.

They not only heard but also believed her. On October 27, 2008, nearly a year after the case began, the justices in the ECOWAS court issued their decision: the government of Niger had failed to protect Hadijatou Mani from slavery and was wrong to say there were customary practices that made slavery acceptable. She was awarded her freedom, and Niger had to pay the court costs and give Mani a monetary award, enough for her to finally realize her dream.

Impact of the Case

Mani's case was unlike any Niger had seen before. A young woman—a former slave—took the country to court and won. Within months of the decision, thirty more women were released from slavery, and today new judges in Niger are required to review the case and learn the law against slavery before they take the bench.

The trial made headlines throughout the world, and Mani was quoted in newspapers and on TV, radio and the Internet. "Nobody deserves to be enslaved. We are all equal and deserve to be treated the same. I hope that everybody in slavery today can find their freedom. No woman should suffer the way I did," she said in the Anti-Slavery International statement.

When Mani received the International Women of Courage Award in Washington, Secretary of State Clinton described her as someone who "never gave up on herself or on her deep reservoir of human dignity." She praised Mani "[f]or her inspiring courage in successfully challenging an entrenched system of caste-based slavery, and securing a legal precedent that will help countless others seek freedom and justice."

On Mani's return home, she bought a small farm with animals—a place where she could live peacefully with her husband and now two children.

Two years later, Anti-Slavery International invited Mani to participate in an event celebrating the publication of a book profiling women who had been enslaved in Niger. In front of a large audience, Mani recounted her own experiences once more, speaking as she had before the ECOWAS court. She had become a role model for women eager to fight injustice. And today, Mani continues to speak out, inspiring other women with her story and working to end slavery in Niger once and for all. Voices like hers are as important as ever. Though no one knows the exact number of women still enslaved in Niger, Anti-Slavery International estimates that there are tens of thousands.

Mani is also continuing to fight in the courts of Niger. She brought a criminal case against Naroua for illegally enslaving her, and she is fighting for custody of the two children she had with him. This part of her story is not yet over.

Sheila Roseau receives her 2011 hero award for her antislavery work in Antigua and Barbuda from then-U.S. Secretary of State Hillary Clinton.

CHAPTER 13

"Little by Little

Fills a Basket"

Sheila Roseau

A YOUNG GIRL WAS SELLING BREAD FOR A BAKERY in Antigua one day when she noticed someone nearby who appeared to be from her home country. Quickly she approached the woman and spoke quietly to her. The woman immediately understood that the child was in urgent need of help. She knew what to do: she took the girl to Antigua's Directorate of Gender Affairs, the agency that deals with issues related to the abuse of women.

"We are known throughout the island for our work, so the woman knew to bring her to us," said Sheila Roseau, the agency's executive director at the time. Her staff listened to the child's story—a story of how lies, trickery and poverty worked together to bring a young girl to the twin-island Caribbean nation Antigua and Barbuda, where she had no family and was cruelly exploited. (The help the Directorate of Gender Affairs provides to its clients is confidential, so nothing that could identify the girl, like her name or her country, was revealed in Roseau's interview for this chapter.)

A Girl Far from Home

The girl explained that her parents had agreed to let her go to Antigua and Barbuda. They were desperately poor and thought they were giving their daughter a better chance for a successful life by sending her away with a man and a woman who promised to care for her.

The couple assured her parents that they would enroll her in school so she would get the skills she needed to provide for her relatives back home. They owned two businesses where she would help out, and she would be like family, even calling the woman "auntie" and the man "uncle." The opportunity sounded good to the parents, but it turned out to be too good to be true.

The girl had no time for school because every day was a working day. "She had to work in the bakery and sell the goods," Roseau said. "She had to clean the house and go to work in their other business. Sometimes she was so tired, but she was unable to sleep until her auntie, as she called her, was ready for bed because she had to make sure everything was fine and make sure her auntie was comfortable."

This was the routine until one Saturday, when the man—the so-called uncle—took her to the other business to work. Once there, he raped her. When the girl returned with him to the bakery, she told the auntie what had happened. The older woman accused her of lying and beat her, leaving her skin badly marked. She then ordered the girl to go out and sell baked goods, as if nothing had happened. That's when the youngster spotted the woman from her home country.

Escape

Although the girl had never met this woman, she instinctively felt she could trust her. She told the stranger what had happened, and the woman took her directly to Roseau's office. As executive director of the Gender Affairs office, Roseau promotes fair and equal treatment of both women and men. People contact the directorate when problems arise—a woman is beaten at the hands of her boyfriend, a qualified woman is not hired for a job that goes to an unqualified man, a worker does not get paid for the job he completes or a woman is raped. In this case, Roseau's immediate task was to make the child safe and comfortable so she could recover from her ordeal. Later, she and her staff would decide how to provide for her long-term care.

Helping the girl was their priority, but they also had to consider taking legal action against the girl's abductors. All of this required more information than they could gather on their own. They talked to the child and worked with the social services department, child protection services, volunteer coordinators, the police and even an airline. "The social services department in Antigua spoke to the social services department in her native land, and an airline provided a free ticket so someone from Antigua's office could visit the parents and get the full story," Roseau said. In the end, the girl stayed in Antigua and Barbuda, where she was placed with a foster family, educated and protected.

Authorities were able to arrest the uncle for raping the girl, but there was nothing they could do about the auntie. In Antigua and Barbuda at that time, there were no laws to protect people from human trafficking. Even worse, Roseau learned that the woman had mistreated other children in the same way—making young girls work at the couple's businesses without pay, without schooling and without proper care. "Our concern was that this not happen to any other child," Roseau said.

Adult Victims

Over the next few years, Roseau did not meet any other children who were tricked into coming to Antigua, but she did meet some adults. "One young lady from a very poor background saw an advertisement in an online paper about being a dancer. She was basically doing things just to survive in her home country and saw this as an opportunity to earn some money," Roseau said. At first things went well. The employer paid for her airline ticket and provided her with accommodations in Antigua. He made her give him her passport, but even then, she didn't question him.

The work was hard, but she remained hopeful. "She was told that she wouldn't be paid a salary," Roseau said. "She had to work seven nights a week as a pole dancer in a nightclub and would have to depend on tips for her living. And then she had to repay the cost of her ticket and for her accommodations." Every penny she earned went to the people who'd brought her to Antigua. She would have to find money someplace else to pay for food and other expenses.

Soon, her situation began to go from bad to worse. The first rooms the woman got were fine, but they were temporary and she was eventually moved. The new place was filthy and ramshackle, and it depressed her. She was desperate to get away, but without her passport she could not travel. Someone told her about the Gender Affairs Directorate, which helped her recover her documents from her employer and return to her home country.

This woman's story is not unusual. Impoverished women are often enticed by ads that promise them a glamorous life on the beautiful Caribbean islands of Antigua and Barbuda. Hopeful women have come from near (Jamaica, Dominica, Guyana and St. Lucia) and far (the Philippines, the Middle East, Russia and China). "They come here knowing that they are going to dance in nightclubs, and they do that willingly to make money. But they end up not making money," Roseau said.

Their handlers—the people who bring them to the islands—make the women pay them back for their plane tickets and their rent. The women also need to buy food, clothes, toiletries, makeup and other incidentals. They dance every night without a break, even when they're sick. If they don't go to work, their handlers increase the amount of money they "owe." The tips from dancing do not provide enough to repay their debt, so the women are forced to find other sources of income. Because of the hours they work, the places they work and the people they know, they generally see no alternative but to become sex workers.

Although the women come to the islands freely, the people who hire them don't tell them about the money they will owe or the additional work they will have to do to earn it. These women are victims of human trafficking. It is the most common form of slavery in the world today.

Roseau and her staff members usually learn about a trafficking victim when the woman's situation becomes so bad that she runs away. It takes courage to do that because the handlers are often brutal and threaten to hurt the women if they try to leave. Men are also trafficked into Antigua and Barbuda, usually to work in agriculture or construction. On farms and building sites, they live in isolated areas, far from anyone who could rescue them. They live in fear of the people who brought them and have no money or documents to get home.

Human Trafficking Legislation

Roseau thought Antigua could do more to help the victims of human trafficking, so she organized a training session led by a staff member from the International Organization for Migration (IOM), a Swiss group that has many years of experience working on the problem. At least one person attended from every government agency that was likely to come in contact with a victim of trafficking, as did representatives from the police, labor organizations and the community. After the training, participants formed a group called the National Coalition Against Trafficking in Persons, which would meet regularly.

Whenever Roseau's office encountered someone trafficked from outside the island, her staff notified the IOM, which in turn informed people in the victim's native country so she or he would receive care and assistance upon returning home. Still, Roseau knew that the solution lay beyond finding ways to help victims. Unless word got out that traffickers would be punished, nothing would stop them. The way things were, if the auntie in the first story decided to bring another young girl to act as a slave for her in Antigua, she would get away with it again. As long as the girl's family consented to the trip, no crime had been committed.

Antigua and Barbuda needed a law against human trafficking. The country took a step in that direction when representatives from the IOM notified Roseau that they were working on model legislation on anti-trafficking and asked if anyone from Antigua and Barbuda would like to join people from other Caribbean countries in drafting it. Model legislation is not a law itself because it is not specific to any one country. It is a sample law that countries can revise to suit their needs. The model would become the IOM's way of saying, "These are all the things we think belong in a good anti-trafficking law." Roseau spoke to her government's legal department, and they sent a lawyer to sit on the panel that drafted the model law.

After the international panel had completed its work, Roseau and other members of the National Coalition Against Trafficking in Persons set about designing a law specific to Antigua and Barbuda. They reviewed every sentence in the IOM model to decide which ones applied to their country. Roseau brought to this discussion insight into the victims and the legal process; her education and experience gave her perspective on both.

As a teenager, Roseau had left Antigua and Barbuda to study in England. Her intention had been to emulate a beloved aunt and become a teacher, but as she explored possible jobs, she chose nursing instead. After working as a community nurse, she realized that people needed help in areas beyond physical health, and she decided to study social work. Her interests were broad—embracing criminology, politics and economics—and she eventually earned a bachelor's degree in social sciences and social policy. She was a social worker in England until 1994, when she returned to Antigua and Barbuda. The next year she joined the Gender Affairs Directorate as executive director.

Roseau understood that it is rarely easy to pass a law, even a popular one. She and other representatives of the anti-trafficking coalition made calls to members of Parliament to push for passage of the bill. The process required give-and-take. The coalition members had to compromise on some provisions, but they were confident that once the law passed, it could be improved over time.

The Trafficking in Persons (Prevention) Act, 2010 became law on October 25. One of its aims is to combat trafficking within and across the borders of Antigua and Barbuda. Anyone found guilty of human trafficking can be imprisoned for as long as thirty years, even if the victim agreed to accompany the perpetrator. Had the law been in existence in 1999, it might have made the so-called auntie think twice before bringing a young girl to Antigua to work without pay. Thirty years in jail is a long time.

The law also ensures that victims of trafficking are provided with medical care, a safe place to live and protection against people who may harm them.

One of the provisions that Roseau hopes Parliament will change in the future is the requirement to publish the addresses of safe houses for trafficking victims in Antigua and Barbuda's *Gazette*, the official government publication. "We cannot have them publicly documented," Roseau asserted, "because they are places for protection of the victims."

Roseau's Role

Although most people give Roseau the credit for spearheading this law and advocating on behalf of victims, she is more modest. She uses the word *we* far more often than *I*. "It's always a collaborative approach, working with partners, working with others," she said in an interview. She is reluctant to take credit for promoting the law, and instead acknowledges the work of the National Coalition Against Trafficking in Persons, her Gender Affairs colleagues and the members of the Senate and House of Representatives who supported the law.

But people in Antigua and elsewhere are quick to praise Roseau. In 2011, the U.S. government issued its annual Trafficking in Persons (TIP) Report, in which it named Roseau a hero for her efforts in helping to pass the human trafficking law. "The strength of Ms. Roseau's personality and the depth of her convictions have helped her projects succeed despite working in a challenging environment with serious limitations in resources," the report says. "Yet she remains dedicated, energetic and enthusiastic. Because of her continued leadership, trafficking victims in Antigua and Barbuda now have legal protections."

At the awards ceremony recognizing all ten TIP heroes, Roseau's fellow recipients asked her to speak on their behalf. In her remarks, she remembered the people who are trafficked. She said:

> Even as we gather here today for this noble occasion, a young girl is being told that she can make money to help her family survive by going to a new land and work under the guise of entertainment, a small work group of men is toiling away in a farmer's field to work to pay off a debt that can never be repaid, a mother is being told if she tries to escape her children will be killed and home destroyed. Their situations are so dire and the stories appear endless. As we recognize the tremendous efforts undertaken, let us ensure that we continue to advocate for effective support for survivors. We must continue to be vigilant in all efforts to combat human trafficking.

Roseau knows that getting a law on the books is just the first step. Her agency is educating Antiguans about the law in hopes that victims will come forward, people will report wrongdoing and trafficking will end. She remains optimistic.

"Little by little fills a basket" is a common saying in the Caribbean—and a favorite of Roseau's. "If we all play a small part, eventually we'll get a better world," she insists.

Nina Smith visits a GoodWeave-supported Child Friendly Community in Uttar Pradesh, India.

The GoodWeave label on a New Moon rug.

CHAPTER 14

"The Eyes and Ears of the Buyer"

Nina Smith

I F YOU'RE EVER IN A CARPET STORE, turn over a rug and look for the GoodWeave label. If you see one, you can be sure that no child slaves helped make the rug. You have Nina Smith to thank for that.

Smith, the executive director of GoodWeave International and the force behind the label, wants to end child slavery in the handmade rug and carpet industry, and she is well on her way. Although a quarter of a million children are still enslaved in the industry in South Asia today, the number would be much higher if it weren't for Smith and GoodWeave. In 1995, when GoodWeave was in its early days, there were a million child slaves in that part of the world.

Learning about Ethical Trade

Even before Smith learned about the mistreatment of children in the rug industry, she knew there were problems with how some people were paid for the work they did. She saw the situation up close as she traveled through Central America in 1993. In Guatemala, a weaver in an open-air market tried to sell her some of her goods. Smith couldn't afford them and walked away, but the woman was so desperate that she followed, dropping the price as she went. Smith quickly realized that the woman was asking too little. She'd never make a profit and never get herself out of poverty.

The encounter was an eye-opener for Smith, who came to see that the amount of money people are willing to pay for a product may sometimes be unfair to the people who made it. There had to be a way to persuade American buyers to pay craftspeople an affordable but fair price. She returned to the United States determined to do something about the situation.

Growing up in a small New York town, Smith didn't pay much attention to the world beyond its borders, but that changed when she entered Tufts University, a school near Boston, Massachusetts. One of the hottest topics on campus was South Africa, a country whose minority white population denied basic rights to blacks. Tufts and other colleges had invested in companies in the country, an action that enriched both the colleges and the whites who controlled the South African economy. Some Tufts students argued that the school should protest that country's policies by selling the investments. These discussions made a huge impression on Smith. She studied international relations and even taught a class on the subject.

Following her travels in Central America, Smith volunteered with the Fair Trade Federation, an organization committed to helping artisans in developing nations sell products made under just conditions abroad. Soon after, she worked for a company that sent her to India to help Tibetan refugees make clothes and crafts for sale in the United States. There, she learned the steps involved in taking a product from the idea stage to its appearance on store shelves in the United States. Those steps included choosing the materials, producers and exporters and marketing the finished product to promote its makers and offer them a fair price.

Stories That Inspire

After two years abroad, Smith returned to Washington, DC, where, in 1995, she became executive director of a nonprofit organization, the Crafts Center, and, a year later, president of the board of the Fair Trade Federation. Through these organizations, she met people who worked in fields, on farms and in factories throughout the world. Many were denied their basic rights. Through a powerful magazine article, she learned that a large percentage of the rug and carpet makers in South Asia are children because manufacturers can get away with paying them very low wages (or nothing at all). International agreements say children under fourteen cannot legally work, but these laws are not always enforced and some countries have not agreed to them.

GoodWeave—which was originally called RugMark—began in India in 1994 to free children from those jobs. (The organization's founder, Kailash Satyarthi, was one of two individuals awarded the Nobel Peace Prize in 2014.)

Smith became founding executive director of GoodWeave USA five years later, and today she heads the international organization, which is now based in Washington. Since its founding, GoodWeave has worked to end child labor in the rug industry. Children should be in school with books in their hands, Smith said in an interview, not at work with sharp carpet tools. "It always comes down to individual stories of children." She has more than three thousand stories, one for each child GoodWeave has rescued from forced labor and slavery.

One of these children was Akkas, a boy in Nepal. "GoodWeave has been supporting him since he was freed from a carpet factory when he was about twelve, and he's now seventeen," Smith said. "He's going to one of the best private schools with our support. He's a top student and a top athlete. He just never would have had that kind of an opportunity without GoodWeave."

When a GoodWeave employee met him, Akkas had been working in a small factory weaving rugs for about four months. His day began at three in the morning and didn't end until eight at night, with only one short meal break. He was always hungry. His dream was to learn to read, but his parents had no money to pay his school fees. His father earned a pittance as a rickshaw driver and spent most of it on liquor. Desperate for money, his parents engaged in a practice common to poor people in South Asia—debt bondage. They borrowed the equivalent of about seven dollars from a debt broker in exchange for Akkas and his older sister. Debts like these are rarely paid off, however, because the person who employs the children charges for expenses like food and supplies. It is a form of slavery.

Children may be very young when they start working, Smith said. At first they begin with some of the simpler tasks, such as helping their mothers or aunts spin wool, but at a pretty young age, they are moved to the carpet looms, where the work is dangerous and painful. They sit on hard wooden benches, curled over to lean into the work, and use sharp tools. "They're inhaling wool fibers and not getting proper nutrition and proper places to sleep," Smith explained. "A lot of the kids sleep in the loom sheds right next to the loom and get up [in the morning and] work again. They might work eighteen hours a day, seven days a week." With poor nutrition and little fresh air and sunshine, some children never grow as tall as they should.

A GoodWeave employee found twelve-year-old Akkas during an inspection of the factory. "He would have made carpets for the rest of his life," Smith explained. "He may have had children born into the same situation." When he was freed, he was taken to a GoodWeave facility in Nepal, fed and housed. GoodWeave also sees that children receive medical care, psychological help and education. As Akkas reads and studies, he can now once again dream of his future.

Before Smith met Akkas, she read about Iqbal Masih, a Pakistani child who was an early inspiration for her. When he was ten years old, in 1993, Iqbal escaped slavery and became a spokesperson against child labor, traveling to Europe and America to bring attention to the plight of carpet kids like him. Two years later, he was murdered at his uncle's home in Pakistan. Though no one was ever convicted of the crime, many people believe he was killed by the so-called carpet mafia, people who support the corrupt system that enslaved him.

Smith decided that Iqbal's message had to reach the world. If people knew of the suffering of carpet kids, they would refuse to buy rugs made by them. But his tragic story hinted at some of the challenges Smith would face in building GoodWeave USA.

In the United States

When Smith began at the organization, she was on her own at a desk in Washington, trying to figure out how to make people on her side of the world care about the children at work in South Asia. She decided to tell their stories in two ways. First, she would speak to American importers and get them to agree that they would refuse to sell carpets made with slave labor. Those who agreed would carry the GoodWeave label on their products. Second, she would publicize the label so consumers would know to look for it as a guarantee that the product they bought was not made by slaves. "I thought, 'This will be great,'" Smith said. "'As soon as people find out about GoodWeave, they'll insist on the label.' I thought we'd have solved this problem in just five years. But we faced opposition at so many different levels." One immediate difficulty was that the American carpet industry wanted no part of Smith's plan.

To get the GoodWeave label, U.S. companies had to buy from exporters that agreed to follow GoodWeave's rules, which included not using child or forced labor and permitting surprise visits from inspectors. Exporters that sold their rugs and carpets to companies in the United States might buy goods from large factories in Afghanistan, while the people who ran those factories might hire small shops in remote villages to do their weaving.

Inspectors would go to the large sites and the small, speaking to workers, checking wage books, reviewing production records. If they noticed an empty spot at a loom, they would ask questions to try to determine if a child laborer had been hidden so the inspector wouldn't see him. If the inspectors found a child at work, the company would be issued a violation, and after three violations, it would lose its GoodWeave certification.

But even some U.S. companies that agreed with all the rules were uneasy about the surprise inspections. For people accustomed to running their businesses their own way, the arrangement with GoodWeave would be a big change. Company owners were used to being in charge and not having to answer to anyone. Factory managers also did things their own way and didn't like outsiders telling them how to produce their goods.

In addition, some importers in the United States were uncomfortable drawing attention to the problem of carpet kids. They were afraid shoppers would be so revolted at the thought that slavery existed in the industry that they would stop buying handmade imported carpets altogether.

Smith understood their concerns, but she was convinced her organization was taking the best approach to stopping child slavery. Buyers held the key, she believed. If they demanded the GoodWeave label, they would be telling manufacturers they didn't want products made by children. And the only way to convince buyers that no child slaves were involved in production was to demonstrate that independent inspectors—people not employed by the carpet industry—had checked every stage.

Other Voices against Slavery

Smith's was not the only voice speaking out against child labor in the 1990s. In the U.S. Senate in 1992, Tom Harkin introduced a bill to forbid the sale of products made by children. The law did not pass, but his efforts awakened people to the problem.

Even earlier, in 1987, Stephanie Odegard formed a business importing rugs from Nepal. "When I started my business, I was trying to bring child labor problems to the forefront," she said in a telephone interview. She was the first American rug importer to sign with GoodWeave, and for a time, the carpets from the Stephanie Odegard Collection were the only ones carrying the organization's label.

When Smith joined GoodWeave, she and Odegard visited companies together to recruit them to the cause. It wasn't easy. At first, Odegard thought importers did not want to sign with GoodWeave because they would have to pay a small amount to help fund the organization. Later, she concluded that they wanted exporters to be able to keep using child labor because it's cheap or free. "Traditional importers," she said, "want the profit that they can make when the carpet is made by a child."

Although some older companies that had been in the business a long time still resisted change, others started signing on. As of 2013, GoodWeave had licenses with 120 companies around the world. "It's a powerful moment when an importer says, 'I want that label on my carpet,'" Smith said. "It turns 'child-slave-free' into a market requirement, just like the size of the carpet, its color and quality."

Inspectors at Work

Today, GoodWeave has teams of local inspectors in each of the three countries in which it operates—India, Nepal and Afghanistan. When inspectors show up for work in the morning, they learn where they will go that day. Since the sites are as much a surprise to them as they are to the owners and managers, the inspectors can't be bribed to reveal that they're coming. The element of surprise ensures that businesses haven't cleaned up for the inspection and the inspectors see them the way they operate every day.

Sometimes inspectors meet managers who refuse to let them in. That's a violation of the agreement with GoodWeave, and the exporter will be told it must cut ties with the manufacturer if it wishes to keep its certification. "GoodWeave is the eyes and ears of the buyer," Smith said.

Wherever they go, inspectors check for the same conditions and fill out the same forms. GoodWeave insists that inspectors be locals who understand the customs of the country. They meet with factory owners and talk with workers about conditions in the factories, as well as children's rights and safety concerns. If they see a child laborer, they try to free the child immediately, but occasionally one will be too scared to leave with the inspector. "A lot of the training for our inspectors is for them to understand how to talk to children," said Smith. "They will gently but firmly put their arm on a child's back, in a way to make the child feel safe." It's unusual for a child to refuse to leave, but if that happens, the inspector will keep coming back until the child feels ready to go.

The fees that companies pay GoodWeave go largely toward education and health care for the rescued children. GoodWeave does not run its centers for children on its own. It works with established schools and social service organizations in the countries and communities in which it operates. As often as possible, the organization reunites the children with their families. It also ensures that each child goes to school until grade ten or age eighteen, whichever comes first, and representatives continue to visit the home to make sure that the parents and the child get the help they need so the family doesn't feel compelled to return the child to work. GoodWeave's philosophy is that education is the key to a good future, and the organization tries to free families from reliance upon their children's labor.

GoodWeave provides an education to each rescued child, but its goal is greater than that. It wants to change the thinking that permits generation after generation of children to perform low-wage labor. Children who sit at looms are likely to grow up and have children who sit at looms, but children who get an education will have more options in life. They are more likely to have children who also become educated, and those children in turn will have more choices. That is one of the philosophies of GoodWeave: education is important because it ends the cycle of poverty.

People Want Change

GoodWeave matches its educational programs to the needs of the country in which it's operating. In Afghanistan, for example, carpet weaving is a huge industry, employing millions of people. All the inspectors are women because most of the carpet weaving is done by women and children in their homes. A Good-Weave program there, called Weaving Opportunities, trains women in production, design and management so that they can advance to better jobs in the rug industry. While the women are training in one place, their young children are kept safe in a GoodWeave childcare center.

GoodWeave also helps older children get an education in Afghanistan. Some Afghan people oppose sending girls to school, so when GoodWeave began to work in the country, it decided to start very small, assigning one teacher to one home to teach one girl. When the teacher showed up at the house on the first day, she found not one but thirteen girls, all ready to learn. Smith found out about this when she received an email marked "Confidential" with a picture of thirteen girls seen from behind, their faces hidden in case the picture got in the wrong hands. "Tears came to my eyes when I saw it," Smith said. "You try to provide help in ways appropriate to the situation, and [then] really good things can happen. People in these communities want change."

In time, Smith hopes GoodWeave will expand beyond India, Nepal and Afghanistan to other countries that produce handmade rugs and carpets, including China, Morocco and Egypt. But wherever GoodWeave goes, it will not rush in. GoodWeave staffers look for local organizations they can work with because they know there are no quick solutions to ending forced labor and child slavery. They must work with teachers, social workers and others who want to see an end to child labor in their own countries.

While GoodWeave has already rescued 3,700 children from slavery and helped prevent hundreds of thousands of others from being drawn into it, there is still much more work to be done. That's why the organization continues to educate Americans about carpet kids. Their freedom will come when buyers in North America demand that their products not be made by slaves. Stories about GoodWeave have appeared in prominent newspapers and magazines, as well as on national TV. The organization even has a traveling photo exhibit featuring pictures of many of the children it has freed. Some of the pictures, together with the children's stories, are also available on GoodWeave's website.

Children in North America can help too, Smith said. Awareness programs in schools send the message from kids to their parents. "When their mother goes to buy a rug and she asks the person in the store, 'Who made this, and where did it come from?' it really makes an impact when the salesperson realizes that she lost a sale because she didn't have credible assurance that a child's fingers did not weave [the rug]."

Change comes slowly, but it *will* come when everyone pays attention to who is making the products.

AFTERWORD

"The Sensitive Nature
of Woman"

WHEN ELIZABETH FREEMAN WENT TO COURT in Massachusetts in 1781, she struck a major blow against slavery: the court agreed that under the new state constitution, all people were free and equal. In 2007, when Hadijatou Mani went to court in Africa, she also forced her government to live up to its own laws guaranteeing her freedom. For over two centuries, women have acted courageously—often at great risk—to fight for freedom.

Of the fourteen women abolitionists profiled here, almost half were slaves themselves. Freeman and Mani fought for their own freedom and, in the process, set legal precedents for others. Ellen Craft, Harriet Tubman, Timea Nagy and Micheline Slattery began by freeing themselves but went on to advocate for others, both men and women.

In the earliest years of the fight against slavery in Britain and the United States, outspoken women were seen as brazen. The reading public wouldn't take a woman's voice seriously, so Elizabeth Heyrick published most of her pamphlets anonymously. Ellen Craft may have carried out a harrowing escape from slavery, but she still had to remain silent while her husband promoted their cause in speeches before the British public. If there was one thing the actress and writer Frances Anne Kemble knew how to do to perfection, it was to express herself in public, but her proslavery husband muzzled her for decades. Even Harriet Beecher Stowe, whose novel *Uncle Tom's Cabin* did more than any other written work to ignite antislavery sentiment in America, could not speak publicly in Britain. That would have been unladylike.

Undaunted, women abolitionists insisted that they had a unique role to play. It is true, argued Heyrick, that "we have no voice in the senate, no influence in public meetings," but "[t]o the hearts and consciences of our own sex, at least, we have unlimited access."

Abolitionist women also made a virtue of what they saw as peculiarly feminine traits. To Heyrick, it was "the sensitive nature of woman" that made her recoil at slavery, which destroys families and degrades women. To Stowe, white mothers were capable of instant empathy with slave mothers, whose children are wrenched away from them on the auction block. The female slaves on Kemble's husband's plantations trusted her with their sorrows—the painful recovery from childbirth, the deaths of children. Alice Seeley Harris urged Englishwomen to take up the cause of their Congolese sisters because the suffering in King Leopold's Congo was borne disproportionately by women, with whom they had a natural empathy.

While women were agitating against slavery, they were also campaigning for women's rights, and by the end of the nineteenth century, they had noticeably more freedom. In 1898, Harris could accompany her missionary husband to Africa as an equal partner. Kathleen Simon could publish a well-received book on world slavery and speak about it in Britain and the United States. By the 1940s, Fredericka Martin was testifying to a U.S. congressional committee about the exploitation of the Pribilof Aleuts.

Today, women often take a leading role in organizations and government agencies that work to end various forms of slavery. Timea Nagy came out of her ordeal as a sex slave in Canada to found her own victim services organization and collaborate with a member of Parliament to pass anti-trafficking legislation. Through her commitment to women's equality in the Directorate of Gender Affairs of Antigua and Barbuda, Sheila Roseau helped shape her nation's first anti-trafficking law. Moved by the plight of child carpet slaves, Nina Smith founded GoodWeave USA.

What Can You Do?

Women today in much of the world can be as outspoken as men. But there's another change that's taking place—young people are working to end slavery. And there's a lot of work to do.

It's hard to estimate how many people are enslaved in our world, but the American antislavery organization Free the Slaves estimates it's as many as twenty-seven million. In this book, you've read about trafficked women, carpet kids with eighteen-hour workdays, and children forced to work in bakeries and as *restavecs*. Slaves do many other kinds of work today—picking fruits and vegetables, making mud bricks, sewing stuffed toys and much more. GoodWeave's Nina Smith believes we can all help end slavery by being smart consumers. When you go into a store, you can ask the salesperson where any product was produced and who worked on it. Another way to help is to visit the websites of today's antislavery organizations to learn about modern-day slavery and the actions you can take. Here are a few:

Free the Slaves (in the United States): www.freetheslaves.net
Anti-Slavery International (in England): www.antislavery.org
Alliance Against Modern Slavery (in Canada):
    www.allianceagainstmodernslavery.org
GoodWeave: www.goodweave.org

One organization that suggests special projects for young people is Free the Children. It was founded after a Canadian seventh-grade student named Craig Kielburger read about the murder of Iqbal Masih, the event that also motivated GoodWeave's Nina Smith. The organization Kielburger began has offices in Canada, the United States and the United Kingdom. Its website is www.freethechildren.com.

One of the most important actions for young abolitionists today, as it was for abolitionists of yesterday, is to spread the word. Let people know that slavery still exists.

SELECTED SOURCES

We have listed many of the sources we used, but not all. Under "Major Sources" we cite those that provided the greatest amount of information, and under "Other Sources" are many that we found helpful. Most of the online publications are easily accessible. Simply search by title or author's name at the website given or through Google. In a few cases, we include more detailed directions on where to search and where to click.

Chapter 1. Elizabeth Freeman: *"To Stand One Minute on God's Earth a Free Woman"*

Major Sources

Massachusetts Historical Society website, www.masshist.org. Search for "African Americans and the End of Slavery in Massachusetts" and at that page click on "The Legal End of Slavery in Massachusetts."

Catharine Sedgwick [misspelled as Sedgewick], "Slavery in New England," *Bentley's Miscellany*, vol. 34 (1853), pp. 417–424. Online through Google Books, http://books.google.com. Search for "*Bentley's Miscellany* vol. 34" and then by article title.

Other Sources

Robin Kadison Berson, *Marching to a Different Drummer: Unrecognized Heroes of American History* (Greenwood Press, 1994).

Theodore Sedgwick Jr., *The Practicability of the Abolition of Slavery* (February 1831). Online through Internet Archive, https://archive.org, and search by title.

Jon Swan, "The Slave Who Sued for Freedom," *American Heritage*, vol. 41 (March 1990). Online at www.americanheritage.com.

Chapter 2. Elizabeth Heyrick: *"No Middle Way"*

Major Sources

Shirley Aucott, *Elizabeth Heyrick 1769 to 1831: The Leicester Quaker Who Demanded the Immediate Emancipation of Slaves in the British Colonies* (Gartree Press, 2007). (It is for sale through the Leicester County Council [England] website, www.leics.gov.uk.)

Elizabeth Heyrick, *Immediate, Not Gradual Abolition, Appeal to the Hearts and Consciences of British Women* and *Apology for Ladies' Antislavery Societies.* Online through the Cornell University Library, http://ebooks.library.cornell.edu. Click on "Samuel May Anti-Slavery Collection" and then click on "Search the Collection." Click on "Browse," choose "Sorted by Author" and click on "H" to find titles by Elizabeth Heyrick.

Other Sources

John Howard Hinton, *Memoir of William Knibb: Missionary in Jamaica* (1849). Online through Internet Archive, https://archive.org.

Adam Hochschild, *Bury the Chains: Prophets and Rebels in the Fight to Free an Empire's Slaves* (Houghton Mifflin, 2005).

Clare Midgely, *Women against Slavery: The British Campaigns, 1780–1870* (Routledge, 1992).

Quakers in the World website, www.quakersintheworld.org.

"Women Arise" and "Forward Sisters," free flyers. Online through the Leicestershire County Council, www.leics.gov.uk.

Chapter 3. Ellen Craft: *"I Had Much Rather Starve in England, a Free Woman"*

Major Sources

William and Ellen Craft, *Running a Thousand Miles for Freedom; or, the Escape of William and Ellen Craft from Slavery.* Online through Documenting the American South, http://docsouth.unc.edu.

Barbara McCaskill, "'Yours Very Truly': Ellen Craft—The Fugitive as Text and Artifact," *African American Review*, vol. 28, no. 4 (1994), pp. 509–529.

Dorothy Sterling, *Black Foremothers: Three Lives* (Feminist Press, 1993).

Other Sources

Elizabeth F. Chittenden, *Profiles in Black and White: Stories of Men and Women Who Fought against Slavery* (Scribner's, 1973).

Daily Evening Telegraph, Philadelphia. January 18, 1867, p. 8. Online through the Library of Congress, http://chroniclingamerica.loc.gov.

Paul Jefferson, ed., *The Travels of William Wells Brown, Including the Narrative of William Wells Brown, a Fugitive Slave and the American Fugitive in Europe. Sketches of Places and People Abroad* (Markus Wiener, 1991).

Clare Midgely, *Women against Slavery: The British Campaigns, 1780–1870* (Routledge, 1992).

C. Peter Ripley, ed., *The Black Abolitionist Papers*, vol. 1 (University of North Carolina Press, 1985).

Shirley J. Yee, *Black Women Abolitionists: A Study in Activism, 1828–1860* (University of Tennessee Press, 1992).

Chapter 4. Harriet Tubman: *"I Was Free, an' They Should Be Free"*

Major Source

Kate Clifford Larson, *Bound for the Promised Land: Harriet Tubman: Portrait of an American Hero* (Random House, 2004).

Other Sources

Sarah H. Bradford, *Scenes in the Life of Harriet Tubman* (Ayer Company, 1988). Reprint of first full biography of Tubman, originally published in 1869.

William Wells Brown, "Moses," in *The Rising Son: or, The Antecedents and Advancement of the Colored Race* (A.G. Brown & Company, 1871), pp. 536–539. Online through Internet Archive, https://archive.org/details/risingsonorantec00brow.

Ednah Dow Cheney, "The Black Moses," *The Freedmen's Record* (March 1865), pp. 34–38. Online through http://babel.hathitrust.org. Search for "The Freedmen's Record," then "Moses."

Rosa Belle Holt, "A Heroine in Ebony," *The Chautauquan: A Monthly Magazine*, V. XXIII, New Series, V. XIV (April 1896 to September 1896), pp. 459–462.

Jean M. Humez, *Harriet Tubman: The Life and the Life Stories* (University of Wisconsin Press, 2003).

Milton C. Sernett, *Harriet Tubman: Myth, Memory, and History* (Duke University Press, 2007).

Emma P. Telford, "Harriet: The Modern Moses of Heroism and Visions," ca. 1905. Dictated by Harriet Tubman. Courtesy of the Cayuga Museum of History and Art, Auburn, NY.

Chapter 5. Harriet Beecher Stowe: *"I Will Write Something. I Will If I Live"*

Major Sources

Henry Louis Gates Jr. and Hollis Robbins, eds., *The Annotated Uncle Tom's Cabin* (Norton, 2007).

Joan D. Hedrick, *Harriet Beecher Stowe: A Life* (Oxford University Press, 1994).

Uncle Tom's Cabin and American Culture website, http://utc.iath.virginia.edu.

Other Sources

Susan Belasco, ed., *Stowe in Her Own Time* (University of Iowa Press, 2009).

Patricia R. Hill, "*Uncle Tom's Cabin* as a Religious Text" (2007). Online at http://utc.iath.virginia.edu/interpret/exhibits/hill/hill.html.

Stephen A. Hirsch, "Uncle Tomitudes: The Popular Reaction to 'Uncle Tom's Cabin,'" *Studies in the American Renaissance* (1978), pp. 303–330.

Eric J. Sundquist, ed., "Introduction," *New Essays on* Uncle Tom's Cabin (Cambridge University Press, 1986), pp. 1–44. Also see this anthology for Richard Yarborough's "Strategies of Black Characterization in *Uncle Tom's Cabin* and the Early Afro-American Novel," pp. 45–84.

Chapter 6. Frances Anne Kemble: *"So Grievous a Sin against Humanity"*

Major Sources

Catherine Clinton, *Fanny Kemble's Civil Wars* (Simon and Schuster, 2000).

William Dusinberre, *Them Dark Days: Slavery in the American Rice Swamps* (Oxford University Press, 1996), especially pp. 213–273.

Frances Anne Kemble, *Journal of a Residence in America*. Online through Internet Archive, https://archive.org, and search by title. Also, *Journal of a Residence on a Georgian Plantation* and *Records of a Girlhood*. Online through Project Gutenberg, www.gutenberg.org.

Other Sources

Margaret Armstrong, *Fanny Kemble: A Passionate Victorian* (Macmillan, 1938).

John A. Scott, ed., *Journal of a Residence on a Georgian Plantation in 1838–1839*, by Frances Anne Kemble (Brown Thrasher, 1984).

Mortimer Thompson, *What Became of the Slaves on a Georgia Plantation?* (1863). Online through New York University Undercover, http://dlib.nyu.edu/undercover.

Chapter 7. Alice Seeley Harris: *"They Are Women As You and I Are"*

Major Sources

Kevin Grant, *A Civilised Savagery: Britain and the New Slaveries in Africa, 1884–1926* (Routledge, 2001).

Adam Hochschild, *King Leopold's Ghost: A Story of Greed, Terror, and Heroism in Colonial Africa* (Houghton Mifflin, 1998).

Other Sources

Harris Letters:

Alice Harris to Mons. Van Calcken, May 15, 1904. Mss. Brit. Emp. S19, D5/10.

John Harris to Dr. Harry Guinness, May 19, 1904. Mss. Brit. Emp. S19, D5/9.
    Both available from Bodleian Library, Rhodes House, Oxford University.

Alice Harris to E.D. Morel, December 30, 1905. LSE/Morel/F9/3. Available from British
    Library of Political and Economic Science, London School of Economics.

Alice Seeley Harris, *Enslaved Womanhood of the Congo: An Appeal to British Women* (Congo
    Reform Association, ca. 1908), and the transcript of Mary-Jean Hasler's 1970 BBC Radio
    interview with Harris. Both available through Anti-Slavery International, London.

John Harris, *Botofé Bo Le Iwa (Rubber Is Death): The Story of the Bongwonga Rubber Collectors*
    (Regions Beyond Missionary Union, 1906).

John Harris and Alice Seeley Harris, *The Camera and the Congo Crime* (Congo Reform
    Association, 1906). Available from Lambeth Palace Library, London.

Chapter 8. Kathleen Simon: *"To Wipe the Dark Stain of Slavery from the Face of the World"*

Major Sources

Susan D. Pennybacker, *From Scottsboro to Munich: Race and Political Culture in 1930s Britain*
    (Princeton University Press, 2009), especially pp. 103–145.

Kathleen Simon, *Slavery* (Hodder and Stoughton, 1930).

Kathleen Simon's letters to W.E.B. Du Bois. Online through the W.E.B. Du Bois Library,
    University of Massachusetts Amherst, http://credo.library.umass.edu.

Other Sources

Anti-Slavery Reporter and Aborigines' Friend (July 1929, October 1929, January 1930, October
    1933, and January 1934).

David Dutton, *Simon: A Political Biography of Sir John Simon* (Aurum Press, 1992).

Suzanne Miers, "Britain and the Suppression of Slavery in Ethiopia," *Slavery and Abolition,*
    vol. 18, no. 3 (December 1997), pp. 257–288.

Sybil Oldfield, "Simon [nee Harvey], Dame Kathleen Rochard, Viscountess Simon," in *Women
    Humanitarians: A Biographical Dictionary of British Women Active Between 1900–1950* (Continuum, 2001).

Chapter 9. Fredericka Martin: *"We Have a Lot of Social Problems Here"*

Major Sources

Dorothy Jones, *Century of Servitude* (University Press of America, 1982). Online through Arctic Circle. Search Google by author and title.

Fredericka Martin, *Before the Storm: A Year in the Pribilof Islands, 1941–1942*, edited by Raymond Hudson (University of Alaska Press, 2010).

Fredericka Martin, "Wanted: A Pribilof Bill of Rights," *The American Indian*, vol. 2, no. 4 (Fall 1946), pp. 1–25.

Lisa M. Short, "Fredericka I. Martin" (master's thesis, Alaska Pacific University, 1995).

Other Sources

"Fredericka Imogen Cohen Martin," short biographical entry from the Abraham Lincoln Brigade Archives, Volunteers. Online through www.alba-valb.org and search by name.

Taped interview with Fredericka Martin, by Patty Kastelic (June 7, 1986), University of Alaska Fairbanks Oral History, 90-10-11.

Taped interview with Fredericka Martin, by Ted Ryberg and Ron Inouye (May 14, 1986), University of Alaska Fairbanks Oral History, 86-116-01.

Chapter 10. Timea Nagy: *"Everyone Is Worth It"*

Major Sources

Timea Nagy, interviews with the authors, June 6 and October 21, 2013.

Timea Nagy, *Memoirs of a Sex Slave Survivor* (Communication Dynamics, 2010).

Other Sources

Robert Hooper, interview with the authors, October 22, 2013.

Walk With Me Canada Victim Services website, www.walk-with-me.org.

Chapter 11. Micheline Slattery: *"The Best Way to Remove Shame Is to Expose the Shame"*

Major Sources

Micheline Slattery, interviews with the authors, March 18 and April 15, 2013.

Other Sources

Lisa Chedekel, "Up from Slavery," *Hartford Courant*, January 1, 2006.

Micheline Slattery, "The Journey of an Orphan: In and Out of Bondage from Haiti to Connecticut," in *Enslaved: True Stories of Modern Day Slavery*, edited by Jesse Sage and Liora Kasten (Macmillan, 2006).

University of Central Florida, Global Perspectives, John Bersia interview with Micheline Slattery, October 15, 2009. Online through the university, http://ucfglobalperspectives.org. Search UCF Global Perspectives for "Micheline Slattery."

Chapter 12. Hadijatou Mani: *"I Was Sold Like a Goat"*

Major Sources

Romana Cacchioli, interview with the authors, February 26, 2013.

Helen Duffy, "*Hadijatou Mani Koroua v. Niger*: Slavery Unveiled by the ECOWAS Court," *Human Rights Law Review*, vol. 9, no. 1 (2009), 151–170. Online through Interights at www.interights.org. Search "Hadijatou Mani."

Hadijatou Mani Koraou v. The Republic of Niger Judgment, ECOWAS Community Court of Justice, October 27, 2008, ECW/CCJ/APP/0808. Online through Google.

"International Woman of Courage, Hadizatou [sic] Mani," Trafficking in Persons (TIP) Report, 2009. Online through the U.S. Department of State, www.state.gov. Search "Hadizatou Mani."

Other Sources

Anti-Slavery International Briefing Paper. Online through www.antislavery.org. Search "Hadijatou Mani," click on "030408 slavery case against Niger" and scroll down to "download briefing material."

DeNeen L. Brown, "Women's Courage Takes State Dept. Center Stage," *Washington Post*, March 12, 2009.

Lydia Polgreen, "Court Rules Niger Failed by Allowing Girl's Slavery," *New York Times*, October 28, 2008.

Chapter 13. Sheila Roseau: *"Little by Little Fills a Basket"*

Major Sources

Sheila Roseau, interview with the authors, June 17, 2013.

Sheila Roseau, remarks on release of Trafficking in Persons Report 2011. U.S. Department of State, June 27, 2011. Online through www.state.gov.

Other Sources

Antigua and Barbuda, The Trafficking in Persons (Prevention) Act, 2010. Online through Google.

Sheila Roseau, interview with Shawn Thomas, *Real Issues*, March 26, 2013. Online through YouTube.

"Sheila Roseau," Trafficking in Persons (TIP) Report, U.S. Department of State, 2011. Online through www.state.gov.

Chapter 14. Nina Smith: *"The Eyes and Ears of the Buyer"*

Major Sources

Stephanie Odegard, interview with the authors, August 13, 2013.

Nina Smith, interviews with the authors, May 13 and August 6, 2013.

Other Sources

Leora Fridman, "Opposing Child Labor with Consumer Demand," interview with Nina Smith for Dowser.org, April 14, 2011. Online through http://dowser.org, click on "Archives" and click issue date.

J. Trout Lowen, "The Dark Side of Handmade Rugs," *Minnesota Alumni* magazine (March–April 2007). Online through www.minnesotaalumni.org and search "Stephanie Odegard."

Rebecca Shaloff, "Weaving a Global Society Free of Child Labor," June 9, 2008. Online through www.changemakers.com and search by title.

"Tufts Alumna Battles Child Labor in South Asia," Tufts University, Jonathan M. Tisch College of Citizenship and Public Service (originally published April 2007). Online through http://activecitizen.tufts.edu.

PHOTO CREDITS

Chapter 1. Elizabeth Freeman: *"To Stand One Minute on God's Earth a Free Woman"*

Elizabeth Freeman

Portrait of Elizabeth "Mumbet" Freeman (c.1742–1829) 1811 (w/c on ivory), Sedgwick, Susan Anne Livingston Ridley (fl.1811) / © Massachusetts Historical Society, Boston, MA, USA / The Bridgeman Art Library

Chapter 2. Elizabeth Heyrick: *"No Middle Way"*

Silhouette of Heyrick
© Religious Society of Friends in Britain

Woman beating cassava, Jamaica
Courtesy of the Library of Congress, LC-USZC4-3072

Chapter 3. Ellen Craft: *"I Had Much Rather Starve in England, a Free Woman"*

Ellen Craft in disguise
Craft, William. Ellen Craft: The Fugitive Slave [frontispiece image from Running a Thousand Miles for Freedom; or, the Escape of William and Ellen Craft from Slavery]. London: William Tweedie, 1860. Documenting the American South. University Library, The University of North Carolina at Chapel Hill, 2001.
http://docsouth.unc.edu/neh/craft/frontis.html

Drawings of William and Ellen Craft
Manuscripts, Archives and Rare Books Division, Schomburg Center for Research in Black Culture, The New York Public Library, Astor, Lenox and Tilden Foundations

Chapter 4. Harriet Tubman: *"I Was Free, an' They Should Be Free"*

Portrait of Tubman
Courtesy of the Library of Congress, LC-USZ62-7816

Chapter 10. Timea Nagy: *"Everyone Is Worth It"*

Timea Nagy receiving award
Permission granted by the Privy Council Office, December 5, 2013
Source: Office of the Prime Minister
Photo by: Jason Ransom
© Her Majesty the Queen in Right of Canada, 2012

Chapter 11. Micheline Slattery: *"The Best Way to Remove Shame Is to Expose the Shame"*

Micheline Slattery
© Michelle Guffey/The Augusta Chronicle/ZUMAPRESS.com

A child *restavec*
Photo by Shaul Schwarz/Getty Images

Chapter 12. Hadijatou Mani: *"I Was Sold Like a Goat"*

Hadijatou Mani with daughter
Boureima HAMA/AFP/Getty Images

Chapter 13. Sheila Roseau: *"Little by Little Fills a Basket"*

Sheila Roseau receiving award
Courtesy of the U.S. State Department

Chapter 14. Nina Smith: *"The Eyes and Ears of the Buyer"*

Nina Smith with children
Photo © U. Roberto Romano, courtesy of GoodWeave

Rug with GoodWeave label
New Moon rug, courtesy of GoodWeave

ACKNOWLEDGMENTS

Romana Cacchioli, program and advocacy team manager of Anti-Slavery International, was generous with her time in discussing Hadijatou Mani and patient in explaining the intricacies of Mani's trials. We thank her for her help.

Anti-Slavery International is the direct descendant of Britain's Anti-Slavery Society, which was founded to combat world slavery in 1839. It holds an archive of antislavery publications, letters and artifacts. We are grateful to the staff of Anti-Slavery International for providing us with copies of Alice Seeley Harris's pamphlet *Enslaved Womanhood of the Congo* and a transcript of her BBC Radio interview, and with several of the archival photographs we used in this book.

Thank you to the Cayuga Museum of History and Art, Auburn, NY, for generously sending us a copy of Emma Telford's transcription, circa 1905, of Harriet Tubman's narrative.

We thank Professor Kevin Grant, History Department, Hamilton College, Clinton, NY, for his notes on the lives of Alice and John Harris, and his suggestions for useful sources.

Thank you to Mary-Jean Hasler, who interviewed Alice Seeley Harris for BBC Radio on her centenary in 1970 and shared with us her recollections of that interview.

Thank you to Joan D. Hedrick, Charles A. Dana Professor of History, Trinity College, Hartford, CT, for her helpful advice on Harriet Beecher Stowe.

Thank you to Dr. Karlee Sapoznik, President and Co-Founder of the Alliance Against Modern Slavery, for her helpful advice and contacts.

This book was produced with the support of the City of Toronto through Toronto Arts Council. We are grateful for their assistance.

Our thanks to the people at Tundra Books, especially Alison Morgan and Tara Walker, who encouraged us and lent crucial support when our book was just an idea, and Sue Tate, who managed and guided us through the writing, editing and production process with intelligence, good humor and a steadying hand. We thank our editor, Janice Weaver, for giving close attention to every word we wrote and for asking all the right questions about the text.

INDEX

Page numbers in italics are references to pictures and captions.